1995

Mrs. New,

In memory of my father, Leland R. Long, and my grand-Daniel Moreno. Thank you for your work with Daniel - it was so important to him.

Liz Long Hobbs

WITH STRINGS ATTACHED

WITH STRINGS ATTACHED

The Autobiography of a Music Man

Leland R. Long

VANTAGE PRESS
New York

Published by Vantage Press, Inc.
516 West 34th Street, New York, New York 10001

Manufactured in the United States of America
ISBN: 0-533-10570-6

Library of Congress Catalog Card No.: 92-91162

0 9 8 7 6 5 4 3 2 1

To my wife,
Edna

Contents

Preface

People, in general, may be divided up in various ways. For example, there are morning people and there are night people. There are eye people and there are ear people. There are gregarious people and there are asocial people. There are extroverts and introverts. I am definitely a night person, an ear person, a mixture as far as gregariousness is concerned. I enjoy very much being with people of similar interests, especially those who are musical. I am a mixture with regard to extrovert-introvert tendencies.

Let's discuss the last. I have gone backstage to congratulate many of the greatest musicians. I have been too timid to speak to the person in the next seat at a concert. I have felt painfully shy when speaking to a group, but have held forth, regularly speaking to bands, orchestras, and appreciation classes. I have played my instrument in almost every situation. Sometimes I'm scared to death; at others, the King of Sweden could not upset me.

I have a terrible inferiority complex about some things and border on outright blatant conceit in others. What I am trying to say is that after forty years of music teaching and being before the public as a part of my job in and out of school, people do affect me and I care what they think.

I sincerely hope this writing effort will be entertaining enough to be read, and the name dropping I cannot or will not help.

Introduction

What was it like? I heard my mother ask Lydia Garnet, her guardian after she lost both parents at age sixteen, "What's it like, Lydia, being ninety years old?"

I am not yet that age, but I know my time is limited. I wanted to write down a bit of "what it was like" for the sake of my grandchildren and for the sake of anyone following me who would be interested. I began my career as a music man during the Great Depression. Now, in the nineties, we are experiencing another. Since the Gulf War, changes have been taking place all over the world. In spite of advances in science, we are apparently in a slump educationally and musically.

The symphony orchestra evolved as the greatest of man's accomplishments musically. After four decades of teaching orchestras and bands, also of attempting to bring the rich literature of chamber music into the secondary school, I am wondering what has happened. Have the ideals and accomplishments of Joseph Maddy and Frank Mancini been forgotten?

•   •   •

WITH STRINGS ATTACHED

I
The Whistle

It was in the fall of 1914, a very special day in my childhood, one of my earliest memories. My earliest, I still maintain, was visiting my mother and new little baby sister at the Palo Alto Hospital, transported there on the handlebars of my father's bicycle. Then I was three. My second earliest was a day upon which a historic event took place. Lincoln Beachey, the intrepid early aviator who later drowned when his plane went down in San Francisco Bay, flew over the crowd at the Big Game.

I can pinpoint this day, almost to the hour, by this fact. John Price, Arthur Stuart, and I were playing in the alfalfa field across from Alvarado, known as Faculty Row, on the spot where Stanford Law Department buildings now stand. We were directly across the street from the Prices' and Johnstons', both close friends of my parents, and a short distance into the field. Looking out of the front windows of either house, one could watch Tooney, the red streetcar with side-facing outdoor seats like the San Francisco cable cars, make a wide curve as it moved slowly through the alfalfa field on its trip down past Encina Hall and on through the eucalyptus arboretum to Palo Alto. I am being explicit about the time and location so Stanfordites may identify it if they have lived long enough to remember this location. All that is left at present to give any indication of what I am describing is one tall palm, which was alongside the tracks.

As we usually did, John, Arthur and I had trampled down a play area in the alfalfa field. Suddenly, from the far

1

end of the field, we saw what looked like a gigantic bird rising up and coming toward us. As it came closer and flew over, we saw that there was a man wearing a helmet and goggles sitting out in front of the wings amid a tangle of wires. Except for the man, we probably would have thought it to be some kind of gigantic kite. The sound of the motor assured us that this was our first look at an airplane.

We were shouting and jumping up and down with excitement when I first heard the whistle. (My signal to come home, I should have mentioned, was a shrill referee's whistle, which my mother blew and I could hear for blocks away.) It dawned on me that I had come into the field leading my little sister by the hand. I had promised to look after her. In the excitement of seeing the airplane, I had forgotten Jeanne.

Over by the car tracks I saw her. There she was, sunbonnet and all, picking up pebbles with her back toward the red street car. Tooney was going to run over her I was sure. A thousand whistles went off in my head. I ran screaming toward the car track.

As I came closer, I discovered that the car had come to a complete stop and the motorman was gently lifting my gurgling little sister off the track. She was laughing as though it were all very funny. I didn't think so, though I was tremendously relieved. I took her by the hand and led her over to the sidewalk where I saw Mother strolling with a friend. I handed little sister over.

Mother looked at me and asked, "What on earth is the matter?"

I realized for the first time that I was crying. "I heard you blow for me," I told my mother.

"No, I didn't blow." She looked surprised.

"I was sure I heard the whistle."

Then I told her what had happened. She and her friend hadn't even seen the airplane.

"I'm sure I heard the whistle," I kept repeating.

"Oh, that was just your conscience," Mother replied.

That is the story of why I have gone through life with a whistle for a conscience. It is also an indication of my recognition of and sensitivity to the sounds I hear.

II

Golf and the Steamers

A nine-hole golf course was laid out on farmland just west of Petrikoin's Hill in Greeley, Colorado. Whether the land had been donated by some philanthropist, possibly Mr. Petrikoin himself, or purchased by the city I do not know. I caddied for my dad while he played with college faculty friends, John Finley or Frank Wright. Golf was never Dad's best game. He played tennis much better, but he continued with golf when he moved to Stanford on the West Coast.

My caddying was, in the teens, a distant memory. At different times I saw Stanley Steamer Mountain Wagons, the twelve-passenger version that F. O. Stanley invented. After the streetcar tracks were removed in the early twenties, the steam cars were sold to the city of Greeley by the Estes Park Transportation Company to replace the former trolley cars. They had movable seats to accommodate the immense steamer trunks of the day; scarves and hats the ladies wore, dusters the men. Loose straps on the soft leather baggage compartments dangling in the rear remain in my memory, a visual image I cannot forget. The steam cars often traveled in pairs. With buffalo robes on each seat for passenger comfort, these thirty-horsepower, four-seater vehicles, equipped with chains and curtains (the roofs were the usual fabric as were the cars of that day and the curtains covered isinglass windows) followed the exact route of the former trolley cars.

On a wintry Sunday, with nothing better to do, Loyal Myers and I filled our pockets with a goodly supply of nickels and shivered under a buffalo robe on the backseat as we rode the circular route of Greeley's Transportation System, powered by the thirty-horsepower steam engine developed by the Stanley twins for their race car. In 1906 it had broken the world land-speed record for a mile at 127 miles per hour. The following year, over the same course at Ormond Beach, Florida, it was traveling at 196 miles per hour when it struck a bump and broke in two. Fortunately, the driver, the Stanley's garageman, who drove on both occasions, lived to tell the tale. The boiler rolled down the beach, spouting steam from its thirty or more small, individual tubes, which made the rumor of its blowing up a virtual falsehood, gas-car salesmen notwithstanding.

III

A Turnaround

"Where can I s-s-sit, Mr. Hunt?" Carol Ahlstrand, a very small boy with a saxophone hanging from his neck, a music book in his hand, and a very distressed look on his face, was asking. We were in the training school basement at the college in Greeley. It was my first day in a school orchestra.

Raymond Hunt, a tall man with the look of Clint Eastwood, was the teacher.

"I c-c-can't find a p-p-p-place to s-s-sit," the small boy kept insisting.

I didn't move, because the teacher had just seated me.

Mr. Hunt seemed in no hurry and let the boy stand a moment longer. Then he winked at me before he answered.

"Carol, why don't you try sitting where you've been sitting for the last ten years?" he asked.

Carol, who was diminutive for his age, giggled politely. He slid into the seat Mr. Hunt offered him and got his sax and music ready to play.

I remember this as of yesterday. It was my time to play cello in an orchestra. Nothing seemed to bother my new teacher. I liked him immediately. He was never "uptight" and liked to joke. I'm sure I played few right notes. A first rehearsal could be traumatic, and mine wasn't. The teacher and kids made me feel at home. I was twelve years old. The cello between my knees felt large and awkward, and the strings hurt my fingers. But I liked it.

One cannot forget those beginnings. John Roberts, the fat boy with the big horn—a baritone, I learned later—said,

"You'll catch on." He was good; Mr. Hunt's best, in fact. John's part often doubled mine; he played either trombone or cello parts in the little group; I imitated him. John had played with the Greeley Chamber of Commerce Booster Band the year before.

Loyal Myers, my next-door neighbor, was a clarinet player. He was good, too. It was Loyal who told Mr. Hunt about the kid next door who played the cello.

It was Loyal who conveyed Mr. Hunt's invitation to "Try it. You might like it."

•   •   •

I was in John's father's corner grocery store on the morning when the new euphonium arrived. The store was on Eighth Avenue, immediately across from the campus and just a block from where I lived on Seventh Avenue. The candy counter attracted kids of all ages.

I watched John and his father unpack the gorgeous double-belled instrument. This beautiful creation, a hybrid combination of baritone-trombone, was among the first of its kind, put out by the Buescher Company of Elkhart, Indiana, with four valves, both gold-plated bells facing front, and a burnished silver-plated finish on the rest. Using the fourth valve, the player was in command of the brassy trombone sound or the mellower sound of a large-bore baritone horn.

Before long, John was not only playing for the movies in the Sterling Theater orchestra; he was spotlighted, standing in the box closest to the pit, where Mr. Hunt led the orchestra with his clarinet. Mr. Hunt's departure for Wichita, Kansas, was a sad blow to all of us. Until he left, however, John's solos on the gorgeous new instrument, the light on its gold bell completely dazzling and eye-catching

7

and the heavenly sound rolling out of its bell, completely mesmerized everyone in the theater.

I was immediately captivated by the euphonium, though not at all willing to give up the cello. My parents compromised by allowing me to take some private lessons on the baritone horn from the new band teacher at the college, J. J. Thomas. Mr. Thomas, a versatile graduate of the Dana Musical Institute in Warren, Ohio, took Mr. Hunt's place when he moved away to Wichita.

After "Harmony" Hunt (so-called because he taught that subject in college) left, there were decided changes in the music department at the college. At this late date I cannot recall the exact sequence of their being made.

J. DeForest Kline became music chairman and conductor of the Greeley Philharmonic. A very formal, dignified man, a baritone singer with a goatee, Dr. Kline took the place of J. C. Kendel.

A very dapper handsome little man with a black mustache, pompador, and sideburns, J. J. Thomas, took Mr. Hunt's place as our band and orchestra leader. An excellent violinist and graduate of Dana Music Institute, he became the new concertmaster of Kline's Philharmonic. All of us liked J. J. and his quiet manner. The transition was smooth for our new teacher, although I know that John Roberts missed Harmony Hunt more than the rest of us.

An excellent violinist and theater musician, J. J. Thomas had learned to play a number of brass instruments while in an army band toward the end of World War I. A new set of band instruments, which the college had supplied for him to form a band, came into immediate use.

I joined the beginning band class of Mr. Thomas, took private cello lessons from him, and was permitted to use the new baritone horn owned by the college. Which instrument I brought to my cello or baritone lesson depended on how much I had practiced the cello in the Sebastian Lee method assignment I had been given. I felt that the baritone was relatively the easier of the two. The old Otto Langey method, in which I had my baritone lesson, I considered far more fun. Of course, "Asleep in the Deep" and "When Big Profundo Hit Low C" in the back pages were tunes I could dig. Sebastian Lee's book was largely scales and exercises.

Anyway, Mr. Thomas, for the sake of his band, wanted a baritone player. I was it.

IV

High Drama in a Small Place

"Billy," we would whisper, "tell us about the time when you fell out of the airplane."

Our eight o'clock Latin class was in the venerable red brick Administration Building of the Colorado State College of Education in Greeley. The Training School itself, where I was in the first year of high school, was a similar large red brick building, about a city block away. The white sandstone library, a vine-covered building, was in between.

None of us objected to having our class in the main building of the college, because we could mingle with college students between classes. Besides, it was quiet and dignified, and we felt inclined to keep it that way even if we were merely pretending to be older. Some of our teachers taught classes regularly in the college, and it was a convenience for them as well. During high school I became accustomed to attending college classes for many elective subjects: Geography of the British Isles, Geology of the Rocky Mountain Region of Colorado, Botany, Beginning Band, Band, Orchestra, and Beginning French were all taken alongside college students. All of us in the Latin class were freshmen in high school, and our new teacher, Mr. Laux, had just come over from Paris, France.

We whispered to Billy Laux for an altogether different reason than just to keep it quiet. DuPoncet had come in, as he usually did, about halfway through the hour and was reading his newspaper. That is, he read the paper until he fell asleep. We knew that had happened by the way the paper was spread out over his ample tummy, with some of it

10

on the floor. All the signs were there. Conjugations became terribly dull before the end of the period, and it was far more fun hearing Billy's stories.

"Billy, tell us about the time when you fell," we begged.

Mr. Laux was not so naive as to believe that hearing about his war experiences was our only motive for asking. But conjugations became dull to him also. Besides, he needed to polish his English. With a second glance to the back of the room, he shrugged and launched into his tale.

"Ve waire, how you say, on bumbbing trip to Deutschland, vary, vary deep longe. Ve donna know if we make it beck. Chooste ven ve get beck to France, ve run short of petrol . . ." The plane came in too low for parachutes. It was about to crash. (I remember the details better than his accent.) "I see a haystack. If I stay with plane, we crash, maybe burn. If I jump, I may miss. Have ten seconds to decide. I jump."

Anyway, our teacher was one of those incredibly lucky individuals who had jumped and lived to tell about it. Not many have Latin teachers who are war heroes. We liked Mr. Laux, admired him, and did some work at home, but not enough. We found that out the next fall when we had a new Latin teacher.

•　　•　　•

Catherine Crates was her name. She looked like a flapper right out of Clara Bow's book, or movie. Vive la différence. Miss Crates looked like a beautiful little Greek girl, bobbed hair, spit curl, and all. But were her looks deceptive! Most decidedly. It simply wasn't fair. We started out with Caesar's *Gallic Wars*. But she soon put a stop to that.

"I see that some of you have discovered the ponies in the library," she announced about the beginning of the third week. "Well, it's too bad, because Caesar was a wonderfully exciting writer. But the library is full of those ponies and there's no way to stop you." She looked around the class as though we were all criminals.

"Yes, there is one. You may pass those texts to the front of the room," she went on vehemently. "We shall read *Eutropius*. When we have finished *Eutropius*, we shall read *Cornelius Nepos*. When we have finished *Nepos*, we shall read . . ." By the time she had finished, the entire class was not only moaning but beginning to become ill.

But Catherine Crates was a bright and shining young lady. She grew on us, and we had to go to work. She was not only lovely to look at, she had that kind of throaty contralto voice that thrilled any adolescent male in her class. Within a fortnight every boy in the class was madly in love with teacher. She had satiny olive skin, large brown eyes with long lashes, bee-stung lips—all of it real. On the other hand, she knew how to pour on the Latin assignments, and they were real also.

Miss Crates was, of course, DuPoncet's leading lady in the faculty plays. She was an excellent actress and broadened the scope of the faculty players. DuPoncet was himself a former Belasaco actor. He not only directed the plays but acted in them. *Grumpy*, a play in which he took the lead, was most outstanding, and he was as memorable in his timing as was Guinness in *Dylan*. An original play by DuPoncet, *The Man from Mexico*, was produced on the professional stage one summer in Mexico City and he took the leading role in the Spanish-language production of his play.

What grade did I receive in Latin? Friend Tom Eaton always seemed to get his As—even in Miss Crates's class. Gurd and I got our Bs by the skin of our teeth. We learned some years later that Crates went to Europe to study and married a Belgian.

"Such a waste," Gurd remarked.

DuPoncet? After more than thirty years of service to the college, the old Belasco actor, the man who was fluent in five languages, the actor, the director, the author, the man who, if he had stayed with it, might have been another Guinness or Olivier, was dismissed. Some busybody had poked around and found that his degrees from Grenoble did not exist. Who cared? An impostor? Hardly.

•   •   •

While growing up in Greeley, I was often impressed with the remoteness of this western town. It was a small dot on the map twenty-five miles east of the Rocky Mountain Range, which, like the elongated spine of a gigantic dinosaur, sprawls in a southwesterly direction from the Wyoming border to the southernmost reaches of the state. In those days it was the lonesome sound of a train whistle at night or an owl in a tree in the yard that depressed me. Would this be my home forever? If not, where would I end up? My teens were difficult. Sometimes I cried my eyes out at night over the prospect. It was not that I longed to be back in California so much as I was afraid that I would end up there.

I had reason to wonder. My younger brother had died in Greeley at the age of three and a half. The doctor called it a summer complaint, a kind of diarrhea for which he could find no cure. Life was precarious at best in the early days of the century. Most serious illnesses were the result of burst appendixes or infection from cuts and abrasions. My second-grade teacher, Mrs. Sibley, was an early car/train accident victim. Her funeral, which I attended, was a graveside affair, a typical boothill scene from a Western movie: the open grave, snow-covered fields, a small group of people, scarved and overcoated, but with no other shield from the wind. In my mind's eye I can still see old Mr. Sibley, hatless and bereft, standing beside the grave, his sparse hair and overcoat blown by the relentless wind. I had seen the demolished car alongside the track.

It was Greeley's proximity to the glorious mountains that made one forget the severity of the winters. A trip to Estes Park, through Thompson Canyon, to hike in the virgin wilderness at the base of the Snowy Range, sometimes not to see a soul for an entire day, was a panacea for one's troubles. We availed ourselves of the peaceful serenity of the mountains whenever we could.

At school, the quality of my teachers was exceptional, something of which I was only vaguely conscious at the time. More lasting than the influence of Billy Laux or Catherine Crates upon my life were the combined effects of a number of master teachers, who trained not only us but the student teachers from the college. We had the latter in abundance. Woe to him or her if we, the "faculty brats," didn't get our "passing grade." The stiffly erect state board members audited each teacher's performance from the back of the room. It was surprising how listless and ignorant we could be on occasion. Yes, we realized our power; I sincerely hope we didn't abuse it.

J. C. Kendel, later Denver's supervisor of music and one of three former teachers of mine to become president of MENC (Music Educators National Conference) (The others were Ralph Rush, USC music professor, with whom I studied conducting at Interlochen, and Paul Van Bodegraven, New York University.), and Elizabeth Kendel, J. C. Kendel's sister, my sixth-grade teacher, were both an important musical influence in my life. J.C. and I encountered each other at conferences a number of times.

Mildred Dilling, the famous harpist, had a sister who was my fourth-grade teacher, and Mildred was herself in Greeley for recitals and lectures many times. Teachers who were invaluable in my education include Miss Orndorff, seventh grade; Josephine Hawes and Lucy Neely McLane; Arthur Mallory, math; and Mr. McCorkle, whose first name I never knew, but whose influence I can never forget, it was in so many directions. He was my auto shop teacher, scoutmaster, Sunday school teacher, and what else I can't recall.

Josephine Hawes deserves a special place in any tribute of mine to former teachers. Her English classes were most stimulating. She supervised the school newspaper, the *Herald,* for which I was sports editor, and likewise the annual, *The Bulldog,* which I served in the same capacity. It was she, no doubt, who did the most to prepare me for university work.

In the area of "high drama," my stated topic, there was a triumvirate of lady teachers, Orndorff, Lucy McLane, and Keyes, who cooperated when needed in most of the campus productions. Frances Keyes, dance instructor in my dad's P.E. department (also a violinist in the Philharmonic, which I joined as eighth cellist in my third year in high school), was in charge of the spring pageant. Usually based on the pioneer saga (James Michener was later a professor in the college, and his *Centennial* is based on the history of the place), the pageant could include just anything of theatrical nature, including Shakespeare. Everyone on campus was brought into the picture in some way. Frances asked my dad, for instance, to play "The Wall" in a skit from *Midsummer Night's Dream.*

No one should inflict such pain upon an innocent man as Keyes did on my father, her department chairman. Was she trying to get even for something he had done? It was sadistic. He made his own costume from a toilet-paper carton, inscribing an outline of bricks with black crayon and stapling a branch of ivy leaves to the outside. No baldheaded man could have looked more ridiculous, with his head sticking through the hole in the top and his legs in tights through the bottom.

I remember the lines to this day, he rehearsed them so much: "I am the wall. This is the chink through which to blink," etc., etc. He rehearsed the thing till he got laryngitis and could scarcely croak. Come to think of it, the same thing happened when DuPoncet asked him to appear as a policeman in one of his faculty plays. There were sessions over steam and menthol vapors, all to no avail. No, Dad was not cut out to be an actor. He had too nervous a temperament. I, too, have let that one alone. I don't believe all of the malarkey about acquired characteristics, do you?

V

Local Color

A number of factors were responsible for my making music a hobby and taking up the cello: (1) Dad purchased a hand-cranked Victor phonograph in 1914, shortly after we arrived in Greeley; (2) violinist Fritz Kreisler's Red Seal Victor record of Dvořák's "Humoresque" soon became a family favorite (it also helped sell thousands of Victor phonographs); (3) Mother soon added this piece to her piano repertoire; (4) we were constantly exposed to music, especially Mother's playing of her favorites, "Narcissus," by Nevin, and " 'Neath Sheltering Leaves," by Thome; (5) J. C. Kendel, later Denver's music supervisor and distinguished music educator, produced much fine music at the college; and (6) after Greeley, at age ten, at the Red Cross House in Glen Echo, Maryland, one of my favorite activities was standing outside Mr. Disten's door to listen to him practice on his cello.

To say that I wanted to commit my life to the teaching of high school music was not true. At the college entrance juncture I really wanted to perform, as I enjoyed playing in trios and quartets. When the combination of teaching and performance became possible, after my marriage to Gladys, I realized that if I wanted to make a success of teaching music, the subject I wished to teach, I must make up for lost time. During my first three years in Sacramento and my previous eight years in Exeter, harmony had not been a teaching requirement. At McClatchy High I was suddenly given two more subjects to teach than I had had previously; those subjects were harmony and music appreciation. I was handed the advanced class in harmony—a small group, to be sure, but with several of the best music students in the school. The other class involved history of music, another subject not included in the curriculum of the English major from Stanford. I worked very hard and took some private lessons in piano and harmony.

In 1935, the summer in which my father was dying, I attended San Jose State University, where I attended Adolph Otterstein's class in orchestral arranging. I received his praise and a B grade in a class of music majors, though he explained the curve of his grading me—that I was not on the same level in theory at the start of the class with the others, but I had made up some of this deficiency. He felt that a C did not reflect the advancement I had made. In the days and years that followed, I studied and taught Alchin Harmony at both high schools successfully. Several students of mine made names for themselves in the arranging field. I made an arrangement of a cello solo with band accompaniment that I performed on the Fourth of July with Sacramento's Musicians' Union Band before an audience of approximately five thousand. I chose the piece because the great cellist Emmanuel Feuermann had played it on a national radio network, on the Bing Crosby program. I memorized "Allegro Appassionata" by Sonnallie, made the arrangement, and played it with the concert band during the same week. This was certainly as difficult as any playing I had to do in the six months in which I played with the stage band directed by Bryan Farnon at Harrah's at South Tahoe. Farnon, previously an arranger and sax player with Percy Faith in Toronto, provided a half hour of dinner music at Harrah's: all his own gorgeous arrangements.

Perhaps my taking up the cello was foreordained. Mother often mentioned hearing Langstreth, a San Francisco lawyer, who played cello solos in Palo Alto. She enjoyed hearing him play "Humoresque" on his cello. I recall her accompanying Prof. George Wright, a tenor and father of Homer Lee, a boy of my age. Too bad that Professor Wright went to Washington University in Saint Louis to head the School of Education. I remember him well in a leading role in *The Mikado* and as one of the Wise Men in the school Nativity play.

Shortly after returning to Greeley from the East Coast, I found a cello under the Christmas tree. It had required a trip to Denver, Dad cranking the Model T after jacking up the rear wheels to apply chains for the snowy roads. Then he had the task of fastening on the curtains with the isinglass windows to protect the passengers from the snowy blasts. Then we piled in for the sixty-mile ride to Denver.

At the Bourke Music Company my parents located and purchased a seven-eighth-sized cello for forty dollars. How profoundly this purchase would affect my entire life I did not realize at the time or for many years to come. But that purchase, and meeting my future wife, Gladys, led to a life with strings attached.

•　　•　　•

We were a closely knit little family of four, Mother, Jeanne, Dad, and I. Secrets such as the cost of Christmas gifts were not kept for long. A stringed instrument, the cello, stood in the corner, next to Mother's old Kimball piano as long as I was at home.

Lessons with Leslie Kittle began forthwith. Les was a student at the college, cellist in Ray Hunt's Sterling Theater orchestra, and later a college vice president in Alamosa. He was a big man, mature for a college student. He had played for a short time in the Balboa Theater in LA.

"Let me see," Mr. Kittle said, a frown on his face.

"There is something strange about this instrument." He was holding the cello by the neck to look at it more closely.

His puzzlement vanished shortly.

"This instrument is strung up for a left-handed person," he stated.

After further examination, he noted that it would require a new fingerboard in addition to restringing. The fingerboard sloped the wrong way, opposite to that designed for a right-handed person.

My first lesson had required all of ten minutes. After two more trips to Bourke's, in Denver, the fingerboard was replaced and the cello had new strings. Les Kittle then came again to show me the ins and outs of cello playing through use of the Werner method and a solo book.

•   •   •

Our good neighbors at 1714 Seventh Avenue in Greeley, the Myerses, had two sons, Victor and Loyal. Both had jobs shining shoes, and both played the clarinet. Loyal had joined Ray Hunt's Training School Orchestra.

Loyal and I had been digging caves in the vacant lot between our houses. We also raised a few vegetables there and peddled them in the neighborhood. But our most adventuresome project was a high wire strung from the trunk of a tall cottonwood tree. We fastened one end high on the trunk and anchored the other end to a metal tent peg, which we drove deep into the hard ground. Wooden cleats nailed onto the trunk made it an easy climb up to the wire. A pulley with sling attached allowed us to descend to the ground, supported by the wire. It was a real whiz-ding, the nearest thing to flying that we had ever experienced. The pulley wheel was well made. The bad fall did not take place.

Loyal suggested that I bring my cello over to Ray Hunt's Training School Orchestra, which did not have a cello. Mother had made a nice bag for the cello, doing the sewing on her old White treadle machine. Dad later made a pup tent through the same process, doing the sewing himself. He was very handy with tools and had turned a piece of mahogany into a lamp using the lathe in the college manual training shop at the college.

VI

Noisy Seven

At first there were five of us: trumpet, euphonium, clarinet, sax and drums. I was the noisiest, playing the bass drum for the basketball pep band. Then we added another sax and French horn. I was still playing drums, using a set of traps, but learning the baritone and tuba. Before we were out of high school, I had switched to playing tuba. Other instruments were added to make us the Noisy Nine.

By this time most of us were seniors in College High in Greeley. We regularly traveled on the bus with the basketball team, which had followed the example of the Windsor Wizards and had become champions. Windsor, fourteen miles from Greeley, with only fifty boys in the school, had gone to Chicago and won the national title in their class.

What all of this meant for the pep band was several lengthy bus trips to our northern neighbors, Cheyenne, Casper, and Laramie, in Wyoming, in the dead of winter. Of course we were also playing with the college band, with their series of games.

Regrettably, I missed hearing Pablo Casals play a cello concert in Denver because of having to play for a game. In spite of all of this and other band playing, I became more addicted to the cello than ever. Strings were already attached. During both junior and senior years I was playing in the rear of the cello section of the Greeley Philharmonic, an orchestra founded by J. C. Kendel in 1911 (which makes it older than the San Francisco Symphony). Under J. DeForest Kline we barnstormed the small towns of northern Colorado and played over the new radio station, KOA, in Denver.

Members of the Noisy Seven and Noisy Nine were the envy of their classmates, who cared little for the "long-haired" stuff. Sometimes we were pitted against fifty-piece bands. With John Roberts as our leader and most of our music off-the-cuff, had we known that Bix Beiderbecke existed, we could have possibly been younger rivals of his. He was slightly before our time. Glenn Miller, during his year in Boulder, was a slightly older contemporary to us in Greely, sixty miles or so away.

John Roberts, who played trombone in the Philharmonic, was definitely our leader. Music was a lifelong hobby and New Orleans type jazz his favorite recreation. Fred Rupp, then a small red-haired kid with a "cast-iron" lip, had the brunt of it in playing the lead trumpet. Connie Seastrand, who looked like an undersized seventh-grader, played piccolo and soprano sax. Peterson, a large boy, in contrast, was the alto sax. Dr. Gurd Miller, whose father was a dean of the college, gave Gurdon Ransome Miller II cornet lessons in the old style. I witnessed some of these lessons and heard him advise Gurd to "lay out" for a strain or two during parades, to give his body a chance to recover. Unfortunately, Dr. Miller died after a Fourth of July parade in the same town I mentioned previously, Windsor, Colorado.

John Roberts became Denver's East High bandleader and later supervisor of music in the schools. Fred Rupp, after playing in the circus band of Ringling Brothers, Barnum and Bailey, also went into the school music business. I did not hear of the later careers of the others but recall a chance meeting of a number of us at the Wells Music Company in Denver. I, like a number of them, was in that trade.

My only other contact with John was over the phone

from Sacramento when I was music department chairman at Sacramento High. We were at the Philadelphia MENC convention at the same time but did not meet. His authorship of the *Music Educators' Basic Method for Trombone*, published by Carl Fischer (New York) had been known to me from teaching days. The fact that he introduced jazz to the high school curriculum was stressed in his recent obituary in the *International Musician*, the organ of the Musicians' Union.

What did we play? All of the school songs, the popular songs of the day, and some we improvised, including "It Had to Be You," "Doodle Do Do," and "A Hot Time in the Old Town." John would help me improvise a bass line, sometimes taking the tuba to show me. With a pianist added to the Noisy Nine we became the school dance band. Dorothy Williams and Marion Hall were truly gifted, Marion the more classically trained of the two. Marion won second place in the Young Artists Contest in 1932. After a rehearsal for a dance job, I wrote a letter to the manager of the Stanley Hotel in Estes Park offering to play for a dance there. We were accepted immediately, but I had to back down. The name I had chosen belonged to a band working out of Denver. I turned the job over to them. We were nonunion and just kids.

VII

Don Armagost

Arthur Mallory's one o'clock class in plane geometry at College High in Greeley in 1923 was at the sleepiest time of the day. Several times our teacher himself fell asleep in his chair behind his desk. In fact, I sat next to a student, Don Armagost, who regularly fell asleep in class.

Mr. Mallory, if he noticed, did not seem to mind. But Don had taken care of the contingency of being called on while he was sawing away.

"Lee," he had whispered, "give me a poke and the number of the theorem if I get called on."

Each of us had to go to the board and demonstrate a theorem when it came our turn. Arthur Mallory was very attentive when we did this, except when the practice teacher took over. Most of our classes in College High had a "practice teacher," as we called them, who was learning to teach under the eagle eye of our "real" teacher. Mr. Mallory's class was no exception. Mr. Mallory was also adviser for the Boys' Club and acted the butler parts in the college plays directed by DuPoncet.

It wasn't long before Mr. Mallory asked for Don to demonstrate and Don was asleep at the time. I reached around and poked him and whispered, "Number eleven," as softly as I could. Don was wide awake by the time he reached the blackboard.

"What number was that?" he asked the teacher. Mr. Mallory told him.

"Oh, yes," Don said, and went on to give a perfect demonstration of Theorem Eleven.

I hadn't known that Don worked nights. He was the bellhop at the Canfield Hotel, Greeley's finest. Don found time between customers, especially the late-night ones, to study his plane geometry. Don proved many times how well he knew each theorem and how he had memorized each one by number.

Don provided me with a fine example of how to study my own plane geometry. It helped me to know a classmate who, in spite of a late-night job, could excel. I would have welcomed Don as a close friend, had there been time and opportunity.

Much later, while at Stanford rooming with Don Bryant, I learned of Don's crash into San Francisco Bay. He was a marine pilot in training and drowned, like Lincoln Beachey, strapped in his seat in a plane that plunged into the bay. Sad to report, a number of my generation sacrificed their lives in the early days of aviation. A man named Monahan (I do not recall his first name) was a wing walker. I saw him perform and later read of his death. During a summer in World War II, while working at McClelland Field in Sacramento, I carried a ferry pilot's bag over to his plane. He had just said good-bye to his father and sister, with whom I car-pooled. He never returned, going down in Morocco.

Many were close to death during the war years, many without any remote connection to the service. I had the good fortune to survive those years. My sister, Jeanne, was also lucky to survive, having been in Hitler's Germany prior to the war and in Honolulu on December 7, 1941. I learned of the survival of several of my former students in those years and was grateful for their safety.

VIII

A Career Not for Me

April 26, 1925

Dear Leland,
The haunting melody of your lovely "Elegie" has lingered with me all afternoon. You played it with beautiful tone quality and feeling. I enjoyed it very much indeed.

Affectionately yours,
Elizabeth Kendel

This note from my sixth-grade teacher, Elizabeth Kendel, I have kept these many years. I had played for the Offertory at the First Presbyterian Church. She was the sister of J. C. Kendel, Music Department head at the Colorado State Teachers' College in Greeley until he moved to Denver to become music supervisor in the early twenties. He soon persuaded "Harmony" Hunt to become his instrumental music supervisor there. My first symphony playing was under J. C. Kendel as eighth cellist in the Greeley Philharmonic. I enjoyed conversations with J.C. at the national convention of the MENC in Philadelphia in 1952 and at the California Music Educators Association convention in Berkeley a few years later. At those times he was vigorous as ever and had moved to San Diego to live in retirement.

He, Sigmund Spaeth, author and tunesmith, and movie director Jesse Lassky were speakers at the convention in Philly. Menotti's *Amahl* was brand-new that Christmas of '52. The small boy who starred in its first production and the Met singer who played his mother were both at the convention.

My note from Elizabeth Kendel arrived five years after I was in her class. It was very encouraging to me to have been what I considered scarcely beyond the squeak and squawk stage on the cello and receive such a tribute. I think this kindness from my sixth-grade teacher was very important encouragement at just the right time. Her brother should be remembered, too. He introduced opera in Denver at Elitch Gardens and worked on behalf of music without remuneration in his retirement years.

Maintaining one's expertise on an instrument such as the cello requires many hours of practice, but one is rewarded for his efforts if he performs in public occasionally. Then he is able to measure his progress, and J.C. was also noted around the halls of the teachers college with his violin, caroling at Christmastime.

• • •

Up until my third year in college I had not thought of teaching as a career I would want to have. As I came closer to graduation, especially with the onset of the depression, teaching seemed more rosy as a way to spend one's life. How better can one help people?

• • •

I joined the Musicians Union at age eighteen, in Boulder, and played in the State Theatre Orchestra for silent movies for one year, one Christmas until the next. The Colorado Chautauqua came next and the Boulder Sanitarium, both summer jobs. During my second year I joined the Phi Kappa Tau national fraternity. I also played Sundays and

Wednesdays at the Boulderado Hotel. There was little time for fraternity meetings. My frat brothers excused me and were envious of the eighty bucks a month I was earning. The theater job with Swede Falk and Ham McClure enabled me to escape some of the neophyte hazing that went on.

Later at Stanford, since there was no chapter of Phi Kappa Tau, I lived at home with my parents. My sister, Jeanne, joined the Tri Delta sorority and lived at the house, a few blocks from the family home.

The first home we had in California was in Palo Alto, a large house at the back of a lot on Pope Street (name later changed). It was just off University Avenue close to the bridge across San Francisquito Creek. During my second and third years the family moved to the large duplex on the campus at 583 Salvatierra. But first, perhaps I should introduce to you some people very near and dear to me.

IX

My Unforgettable Parents

Mother's maiden name was Charlotte M. Leland when she married Royce R. Long in 1905. A young Lochinvar from the West, he came back to Dixon, Illinois, and swept the young secretary for the Grandetour Plow Company off her feet.

Of the two, Mother always had the lighter touch and was the lucky one. Her luck ranged from receiving a bequest of stock from her sewing lady, 300 shares of the Van Briggle Pottery Company, near Denver, to having an utter stranger, a member of the cast, hand her a certificate for house seats while standing in a line at a box office with my sister Jeanne in New York. They had just been informed that the play *The Music Man* was sold out and they were enabled to purchase tickets.

With Charlotte there were many such instances. She was not pushy but was still willing to take a chance. At a Hillsborough summer concert of the San Francisco Symphony, as I recall, we were hopelessly bogged down in a line of latecomers. Mother spotted an empty box, then turned and motioned for us to join her. We were appalled at first but, having no other options, followed. We sat undisturbed throughout the entire concert in a box next to the one occupied by Artur Rodzinski, Mischa Elman, Harold Bauer, and friends.

Dad, on the other hand, could never seem to find a parking place unless Mother was with him, seemed to cut himself when shaving even after he abandoned his father's straight-edge razor for a safety, and smashed the large toe of his right foot falling off of his old blue Thor motorcycle. Was there no justice in life?

Of course, such misfortunes were rare and Dad's successes on the athletic field were many. As an assistant coach of the 1907 Stanford track team, he coached Norman Dole (of the Hawaiian pineapple family) to a world record of twelve feet in the pole vault. That was not bad for the heavy hickory pole used in that day and age, before the bamboo pole came into use. I wonder what the modern vaulters could do with the old equipment.

•   •   •

My sister, Jeanne, and I were certainly among the best documented children of the Stanford faculty, even before our parents moved to the campus. Dad was a camera buff during most of his life, often doing his own lab work. Jeanne and I were also among the first hundred registered births in Palo Alto. Dad was the first boy scout scoutmaster in Palo Alto. Among his group of boys was Russell V. Lee, later president of the Stanford Alumni Association, distinguished medical doctor, and benefactor of the community and the elderly. Ray Lyman Wilbur, later President Hoover's Interior Department head and Stanford University president, assisted in my delivery, having been called in by the attending physician in an emergency. Thus I have a unique distinction of having been ushered into the world by the same man who signed my university diploma for the A.B. degree. Dr. Blake Wilbur, his son, an M.D. of distinction, would be my dad's doctor in the last weeks of his illness and would sign his death certificate. Russell V. Lee had been the attending physician previously. All the Wilburs became doctors.

Dad's career in professional baseball had been short-lived because of a cracked collarbone. He worked for the YMCA in Dixon and Peoria, Illinois, and summers at Lake Geneva, Wisconsin, before becoming a gymnasium assistant and student at Stanford. Twice he swam the two-mile distance across the lake as a stunt. He was twenty-three when he entered Stanford University as a special student and twenty-eight at the time of my birth in 1908. It was in that same year that he received his A.B. degree.

I am relating this early history to explain our family's Stanford connection, a deeply felt emotional attachment that was passed down to my sister and me. Our parents moved to Colorado, then to the East Coast during World War I years, back to Colorado until the late twenties, and then back to Stanford. Dad became a full professor in the early thirties and died in 1935.

Life on the campus, where we occupied a house next to the volunteer fire department on Salvatierra, was idyllic for me. The home of Lee Emerson Basset, the public-speaking professor, was at that time next to the firehouse on the opposite side. The tower for drying the hoses and the tub for washing them prior to hanging them out were on our side. One dark night the folks on the sleeping porch heard a commotion.

"So you're from Waterbury, Connecticut?" a voice from the darkness asked. A splash in the water tank followed, with a sound of "gurgle, gurgle." Shortly thereafter the original question was repeated. "So you're from Waterbury, Connecticut?" Again the splash and gurgle, gurgle. The same procedure went on until the folks realized what was happening. The nearby fraternity brothers were giving a boy from Waterbury the water treatment.

I rode my tricycle up and down the sidewalk and learned many years later that I had pestered a couple strolling by. My sister has informed me unequivocally about the malicious teasing streak I possessed at that age. Unfortunately, my apologies have come too late to be of use.

I often joined my Uncle Ollie, who let me accompany him between hedgerows to the post office. Dr. Oliver Martin Johnston was not my real uncle, but our families were close. Aunt Florence, his wife, let Winifred, their oldest, be my baby-sitter. I grabbed Uncle Ollie's forefinger and had to stretch to reach it when this huge man stood erect. I think he was the most patient person I have ever known. I learned more of this when he tutored me in French in later years, using the French text he had written.

Dinners at the Johnstons' were prepared and served by Carrie, a Danish lady, and we exchanged dinner invitations. Carrie lived in their attic for many years. The standing rib roasts and succulent vegetables she served are long remembered, and Aunt Florence set a marvelous table. Uncle Ollie was head of the Romance Language Department at Stanford and in *Who's Who* for his Dante scholarship.

When the Johnstons came to our house, Mother usually had leg of lamb with fresh mint from our garden and mint jelly she had made. Potatoes, Hubbard and summer squash, peas, carrots, string beans, parsnips, and rutabagas were the vegetables served most frequently; strawberry preserves were sun-cooked. Jams and jellies were of all kinds. Those were unforgettable meals at our house and at the Johnstons'. Oliver Jr. invited me to lunch with friend Ray Lyman Wilbur, Jr. Both were still in high school, so I assumed that it was at Aunt Florence's behest. I enjoyed Carrie's cooking under any circumstances.

Other Stanford faculty kids whom I knew through my parents' friendship with theirs were the Prices, Stuarts, and Mosers. The Prices lived next door to the Johnstons. John Price, an only son, became the author of *Birds of the Stanford Campus* and later authored stories for English mystery magazines. Arthur and Elizabeth Stuart lived across the alley from our Salvatierra house. Arthur became a U.S. government employee in Denver. Elizabeth became a Palo Alto physician, with a degree from Stanford Medical School. Henry and Elizabeth Moser are both living in California at present. After a musical education at Juilliard, Elizabeth married Everett Breed, a career navy man, and lived in Arlington, Virginia, for many years. Henry and his family live in Napa, California. Oliver Johnston, Jr., became a Disney animator and is co-author with Frank Thomas, Jr., of a recent book, *Disney Animation.*

•   •   •

In Greeley, where the family moved in the fall of 1914, Dad was head of the Department of Hygiene and Physical Education. He was obliged to coach not only football, basketball, baseball, and track, but the minor sports as well. He and a lady doctor were the entire department the first year. After other coaches were added, he coached gymnastics, his specialty; boxing; wrestling; handball; tennis; and the other so-called minor sports. Hygiene was the academic course that was his favorite subject and one he helped develop.

When Dad returned to Stanford after fifteen years, two of which were on the East Coast, his department had grown to fifteen and the school was on its way to becoming Northern Colorado University, its present name. Athletically, it was in the same league as the University of Colorado at Boulder, Colorado State University at Fort Collins, Denver University, and Colorado College at Colorado Springs.

•   •   •

Dad was a Renaissance kind of man, a nature lover, and a born scholar. He read widely, was interested in many subjects, and was a craftsman especially adept at carpentry, electricity, and plumbing. Single-handed, he added a bathroom to the home on the Stanford campus, and built a beautiful cabin in the Colorado Rockies.

He knew the scientific names of the plants in his garden and raised many that were considered to be exotic for the area in which we lived. He climbed the highest mountain in the Greeley area of Colorado, Longs Peak, four times. James Michener, the well-known author, was on the faculty of the college at a later time. I think it was a pity that they were not contemporaries, because they would have had a lot in common, including a wide knowledge of the world.

It was certainly my own loss not to have been able to compete in athletics in any important way, as one might expect a coach's son to do. My full involvement in music began shortly after my injury in football. Tennis and, since the age of fifty, golf were my sports. I was a sideline spectator for football and occasionally basketball as a member of the bands at the University of Colorado at Boulder and at Stanford during the Pop Warner regime.

Except for a short attempt to learn to play the violin, music in Dad's early life was on the back burner. He was eldest in his family, his father a victim in the Spanish-American War. As a result, Dad worked for nine years in a shoe factory to help support the family.

Many opera recordings in the family collection started in Greeley revealed Dad's taste. Caruso, John McCormack, Harry Lauder, Alma Gluck, Geraldine Farrar, Nellie Melba, and Galli Curci are names I recall appearing on Dad's seventy-eights.

My Dad's early death was a severe blow to me. He was a caring person, and the illness that took him, with modern drugs, would now have amounted to no more than a mild sickness. But I am thankful that my mother was able to enjoy a good long life and was well provided for.

Her concert and lecture attendance on the Stanford University campus in later years led us to make a special declaration: "Mother is the most highly educated widow on the Stanford campus." Her education continued for twenty-eight years after Dad's death.

X

A Career Not for Me—Continued

My father eventually settled on teaching. What he wanted most was to be a medical doctor. He urged me, once or twice, to become a dentist. My lack of interest in scientific pursuits, chemistry, biology, and even high school general science, I thought was a good indication that dentistry was not for me.

During high school and before, I had found literature, from boys' books to the classics, interesting and much to my liking. I spent hours in the library during the World War I years. From *The Rover Boys* to *David Copperfield*, from Horatio Alger to *Moby Dick*, I had my head in books. It was an ideal time for me to do this. Both our parents were fully occupied, Mother as a secretary to Maude Younger, president of the National Women's party in Washington, D.C., and Dad in the army at this time.

From Miss Gibbs, my teacher in the fifth grade in School 54, in Georgetown, Maryland, I returned to the Greeley, Colorado, setting, where my teachers were exceptionally fine. Miss Orndorff, in the seventh grade, gave us a taste for Shakespeare, and Miss Lucy McLane a taste for Lord Byron, Tennyson, and the other British poets.

Then, off to Boulder, where George F. Reynolds, Garland Greever, Mabel VanDuzee, Madge Rutledge, and others gave some more insight into writing and literature. Then to Stanford, for upper division, where I found the foreign language requirement (I chose French) a heavy burden.

My favorite English professors at Stanford were S. S.

Seward, who taught Victorian poetry, a man who loved music and helped the cause of the Stanford Symphony; and William Hawley Davis, with whom I had two courses in Shakespeare. Davis was editor of the university press and was outstanding in his lectures on the bard.

What does one do after graduating with a degree in English?

The thought of teaching others the parts of speech, grading themes, and teaching the same material over and over was very distasteful. After graduation from high school, I had pretty well made up my mind not to teach. When the chips were down, at the end of college, I knew that I would have to teach to earn a living. The advantages and disadvantages of teaching music (that is, band and orchestra) became apparent only after several years of working in the field.

Teaching instrumental music, even in the beginning stages, permits one to choose from a vast supply of instructional material. One is challenged immediately in learning the techniques required in playing each instrument, plus the techniques most appropriate for imparting these skills to others. To teach band, one must know what to select in brands of instrument mouthpieces, reeds, valves, and slide lubrications, and percussion instruments galore and maintenance and repair and playing each instrument can be a life's work. One must actually serve an apprenticeship for many years to qualify to teach the gamut of instruments, from scratch to proficiency. In addition, one must understand music theory and master the art of score reading. If one is to be creative one must learn to arrange and modify existing scores.

To any young person considering a career in music I would say, "Music is as broad as science, because it includes most sciences; the physics of sound is as difficult as chemistry and far more nebulous in terms of materials." Isn't it strange that so many who are untouched by music believe that they are educated? They do not know what they have missed in life.

It was in 1929, at the start of the depression, that I had to make up my mind about what to do. A disadvantage of music teaching, to which I gave little thought, was that it inevitably required hours and hours of extra work for performance, outside of school hours, *with no pay attached.* Those Friday night football and basketball games, those play performances, those parades, graduation programs, and concerts, they are just a part of the job. You are a professional, you know.

XI

Nebulous Horizons

In looking over old picture albums, I often find myself on some high point looking at distant horizons. Two of these pictures, one with my father on top of Longs Peak in the Colorado Rockies and another on the rim of the Grand Canyon near Flagstaff, Arizona, are typical. The backgrounds are hazy, nebulous projections into a distant past, though I prefer at this point in time to think that I was looking into a mysterious distant future. Those were important years, in which I decided on what to make of my life, what to do to earn a living, and what to study in college to make this possible.

What can we know of what lies ahead? History is certainly a great teacher, but at the time to which I refer my background was insufficient to make the decision of what to become. When the Grand Canyon picture was taken, I had been a very sick boy with a limp that might become permanent, an antiphligistine pack around my left leg, and my natural inclination toward active sports completely curtailed. I was a junior in high school, on the way back to Colorado from a fall trip to California. Dad was investigating the possibility of returning to teach at Stanford, a preliminary trip that led to an associate professorship there some three years later.

The trip to the coast was good for all of us. We had seen Theodore Roberts in the prologue to *The Ten Commandments* at Grauman's Egyptian Theater in Hollywood and had ten days in Pacific Grove plus several at Stanford visiting with my parents' former friends. Many of these friends, including the Johnstons, the Ryans, and the Aldens, had us to dinner during the trip. Oliver Martin Johnston was in *Who's Who* for his Dante scholarship and Ryan had the distinction of being the first to develop 2 million volts in the laboratory named after him at Stanford. Mrs. Alden, widow of Raymond McDonald Alden, who had been a famous scholar of English literature, had children my age.

Dink Templeton, Stanford's famous track coach, had said hello to me in the gym. After that no one could touch me with a ten-foot pole, I was so far above the ground. I had been to a Stanford student body assembly and had seen Ernie Nevers and Dud DeGroot, football heroes, in the flesh, while Ray Lyman Wilbur, university president, gave the students a lecture on the evils of alcohol. He concluded with the remark: "The experiment always turns out the same—you persist in making test tubes of yourselves, and the result is always the same." I knew that no alcohol was permitted in the dorms, but apparently President Wilbur was having some trouble. Tall and cadaverous-looking, he somehow reminded me of Abraham Lincoln. "We'll All Go Down to Menlo and Buy a Keg of Booze and Drink to Mr. Volstead Till We Wobble in Our Shoes" was a Stanford song well known at the time.

Harry Maloney, the great Olympic rugby coach, an Aussie who had been a saber fighter in the Boer War, coached many of the minor sports at Stanford, but mainly fencing and boxing. During a trip I made much later in my life to Maine, Henry Varnum Poor, the famous Maine seascape artist whose pictures I had seen in the Thomas Welton Stanford Library, told me that Harry had coached him to a third place win in Olympic fencing. After a dinner at the home of this lifelong friend of my father, Henry presented me with the Olympic book for 1924. It was Harry

Maloney who coached Gene Tunney before his fight with Jack Dempsey and taught him the skill of backpedaling that enabled him to win.

Four years after the California trip, I watched Maloney, then in his sixties, demonstrate his marvelous boxing ability against Fidel La Barba, flyweight boxing champion of the world, who had become a freshman student at Stanford at age twenty-two. It was amazing how limber, wiry, and resourceful Maloney was against the classy young Mexican-Italian. The blows were light, since it was a demonstration bout of three rounds only, but the speed and finesse of each was terrific, with the handsome La Barba exhibiting the skills that enabled him to retire from the ring absolutely unmarked by his profession.

I recall Harry Maloney, his sparse blond hair blowing in the wind, as he and five others carried the casket as the pallbearers at my father's funeral. That was in 1935, not many years later. In 1963, the year of my mother's death, I saw Harry with other patients from a convalescent hospital herding a group of the elderly into the Stanford Hospital for their regular checkups. Before coming, no doubt, he had put those who were able through some calisthenics, as he had done with Stanford students of old. There was a remarkable man, Harry Maloney, one whose respect and goals were very similar to those of my father, and one who lived his beliefs.

•　　•　　•

Horizons became less nebulous for me as time went on and I discovered gradually that music and the cello meant even more than sports. Finishing the university with an academic degree became a necessity after our return to California. Stanford was preordained for both my sister,

Jeanne, and me. But the Music Department consisted of just one man, Warren D. Allen, church organist, and I had no interest in becoming a church musician. I could not possibly major in music at Stanford. Attending San Jose State was a very inviting alternative. It had a fine music school, and I paid it a visit while seriously considering my problem. The following week I matriculated at Stanford, resolving to do things the hard way: major in English and study cello for all I was worth with a member of the San Francisco Symphony, Wenceslao Villalpando.

XII

Cello Instructors

After my eleventh Christmas (1919), my parents had called upon Leslie J. Kittle to give me private cello lessons. He was to come to the house at 1714 Seventh Avenue, Greeley, a block over from the college where he was a student. The seventy-five cents he received per lesson—hard to believe compared with current costs of music lessons—was the going rate. A tall, lumbering fellow with large hands, he was an ideal teacher for me. Later I loved hearing him play for silent pictures in the Sterling Theater movie house orchestra led by Ray Hunt, Greeley's best clarinetist.

Ray Hunt was my first orchestra teacher, later to become instrumental supervisor in Denver. Les Kittle was playing in the Greeley Philharmonic when, as a high school junior, I became seventh cellist. He later became vice president of a small college in Alamosa, Colorado, before going to Hawaii, where he taught in a private school until marrying a widow from Grand Junction, Colorado. I visited him there in his elder years; he had sold the cello and returned to Colorado to live in Grand Junction and was teaching piano.

• • •

Three cellists to whom I owe the most were Wenceslao Villalpando, Colin Hampton of the Griller Quartet, and Gabriel Magyar of the Hungarian Quartet. Villalpando was a deadly-serious teacher, patient to the nth degree, and never satisfied until the lesson was perfect, even if it required three months to get it. Many students of his gave up, including Bess Mannon, a girl who later won scholarships for six years at the San Francisco Conservatory. He was not the greatest of psychologists, but I was mature enough to take the Dotzauer etudes, boring to many students but highly rewarding to those with the endurance to stick with them.

Colin Hampton gave me a knowledge of music, as I studied quartets and trios with him, including the great Schubert Piano Trio in B-flat and the celebrated "Trout Quintet." The essence of playing expressively I learned from Colin, plus some secrets of tone production and ways to improve one's interpretation of either solo material or chamber music.

At the Music Academy of the West in the summer of 1948, I gained knowledge that, from that time forward, was important in improving my playing and conducting. In five weeks at Colby College, under the tutelage of Gabriel Magyar, cellist of the Hungarian Quartet, I felt that I gained musically and technically from close association with this fine cellist. After four weeks of intensive coaching by Gabriel, I performed in a chamber music concert at Colby (Schubert's A Major String Quartet). Through this experience, plus playing under Kutner's baton (second violinist of the Hungarian), I gained better understanding of the Hungarian (Kodály) system. I have great respect for the Hungarian school and a close friend in their great cellist. At Gabriel Magyar's invitation I was his green room guest at several later performances of the quartet in San Francisco and Davis, California.

Comparisons may be odious, but I recall my former teacher Villalpando's assessment, given when he heard the Hungarian years before. "Each member of the quartet is a virtuoso in his own right," he had remarked enthusiastically. Technically they were above the Griller Quartet, specializing in Bartók and the late Beethoven quartets, whereas the Griller was more noted for interpretations of early quartets of Haydn, Beethoven, Mozart and several English composers. Both quartets had the same personnel for nearly three decades before disbanding. Kutner left the Hungarian to conduct and concertize, but he returned to the group shortly before I studied with them in Maine.

Most illuminating was another chamber music experience, that of ushering for the Kolisch Quartet and a festival of chamber music led by Ferri Roth of the Roth Quartet. The Kolisch was unique in performing entirely from memory, and one could not forget the effect of hearing a group with all F-holes of the violins in front, since first and second violins sat opposite at the front. Rudoph Kolisch, bowing with his left hand, fingering with his right, sat on the right at the front. Additional sonority of the four instruments seemed to be achieved with no music stands or printed parts in the way.

One was aware of the extreme tension in the green room of Stanford's Memorial Auditorium. The program consisted of a Mozart quartet, followed by a Schönberg. A furious half hour of wood shedding preceded the musicians' entrance to perform the short Mozart. The Schönberg, requiring perhaps forty minutes to play, was ignored by the audience. The slightest error would have been obvious to everyone in the hall in the Mozart; a mistake in the dissonant Schönberg would be unnoticed by practically everyone.

"Why do you play from memory?" I asked Jascha Veissi, second violinist.

"If you know your music, you should certainly be able to play it from memory," he replied.

I thought of the countless repeated measures in Hayden and Mozart second violin and viola and cello parts when accompanying first violin solos. "Then why don't all of the quartets play from memory?" I asked.

"Maybe that's because they don't know their music," was his answer.

•   •   •

An illuminating chamber music series at Stanford in the 1930s was that of Kathleen Parlow and the South Mountain Ensemble. With a name a bit like country musicians of today might use, this was quite different, a Schubert cycle, including some very great musicians, all now departed from the musical scene.

The personnel, in addition to Kathleen Parlow, Leopold Auer's most famous woman student, included pianist Gunnar Johansen, violist Conrad Held, cellist Willem Willeke, bassist Walter Bell, and cellist Robert Mass from the Pro Arte Quartet. I recall performances of the C Major Schubert Quintet with Two Celli, with Willem Willeke playing the first part and Robert Mass the second cello. Mass played the gorgeous lower part, many passages on the two lower strings, certainly as well as or better than I have ever heard it. Willeke, in his sixties, was in good form, too. It was a memorable performance, with a first-class group.

The "Trout," with Johansen, was equally distinguished. I was relieved to secure Grosvenor Cooper, Stanford friend and pianist, to take my place in the page-turning chore when Johansen asked me to turn pages. Willeke allowed me to carry his cello out to the car, a task more to my liking in those days. He recommended that I learn the Richard Strauss cello sonata, which he had premiered a short time previously. This I managed to do after a decade or two.

Violinist Robert Gross, a six-year student at Juilliard, told me of Willeke's having helped him pick up his broken violin when he, Gross, fell on the stairs. He said, "Willeke was conducting the orchestra, looked up, and saw me fall. He immediately left the podium and came to help me pick up the pieces." Both sat down on the steps and cried.

I noticed that Willeke was out having a cigar during Parlow and Johansen's performance of a Schubert violin sonata. His garter had come down during the previous trio performance, which accounted for his hobbling off the stage. When he turned the corner, he was convulsed with laughter.

XIII
Boulder and a Certain Young Lady

At which juncture in the fall term at Boulder in 1925 I met the young lady who was to play a most important part in my life, I am not absolutely certain. It could very well have been at the first orchestra rehearsal, probably the second week of my first term in Boulder. Her name was Gladys Eleanor Phillips, and the sequence of those early events hardly matters.

Gladys was very pretty, I thought, with a trim figure, naturally curly dark brown hair, and medium/light skin, and wore silk stockings and some makeup. She was nineteen at the time, and I would just turn eighteen the coming February.

I know that I was timid and did not exchange many words with Gladys directly for several weeks. However, during the early rehearsals of the background music for *Erminie,* to be performed in Macky Auditorium later in the fall term, I was assuredly very much aware of the charms of our concertmaster. (Not until I had been coached by Howard Reynolds, her teacher and concertmaster of the Denver Symphony Orchestra, did I learn that the cello and I could be important to her.)

Frank Wilbur Chace, our director, was the university organist. His principal job was to "float" most of the school programs from the keyboard of the Macky Auditorium pipe organ, a superb instrument of its kind with an echo organ as large as many full-sized pipe organs.

Mr. Chace, an excruciatingly thin man, wore thick-lensed pince-nez, with the usual thin black ribbon attached. His sparse brown hair was parted in the middle, and he had bright pink cheeks and a perpetually surprised look on his face. In the 1915 Chicago World's Fair, he had won first prize for his pipe organ playing. He did not stand on a podium and wave a baton at our small group of string and wind players. Mr. Chace directed from the keyboard of an upright piano. A slight oddity about his piano playing was that his feet and legs were in constant motion, as though he were searching for bass pedal notes that weren't there.

While playing the cello part to *Erminie,* I soon discovered that it was Gladys, with her violin, who was holding the group together as much as or more than our professor. I found that I approved of her playing as well as her looks. Rehearsals went on, ending with the gala performance of *Erminie* in Macky Auditorium.

Mr. Chace, of course, soon brought in Margaret Saunders, the conservatory piano accompanist, and then he could pick up his baton. Before long, Gladys and I became friends, not dating in a formal sense, but playing trios for her Christian church Sunday school, Mr. Bartlett's Methodist production of "The Seven Last Words of Christ" (Dubois), and a number of trio requests, one of which, the dedication of the new little theater, stands out in my mind.

Margaret Saunders, Albert Vincent, and Evelyn White were excellent pianists in school at the time. Since I had apparently fallen into the shoes of Gottlieb, a cellist just graduated, I was busy outside my English studies, which suffered as a consequence. This was a pattern that continued for the next five years, two at Boulder and three at Stanford: the struggle to find time for cello practice and trio playing.

Shortly after Christmas, Gladys left for California, not to live in Hemet with Arthur and Hetty, her sister and brother-in-law, and Phillip, their son, as she had done in her last year of high school, but to study with Moenauer in Los Angeles and try her wings at professional playing. It was August before she returned.

In the meantime I had formed my musical alliance with Swede and McClure and played in the State Theater and the Boulderado Hotel.

There was an element of love at first sight, as I admired the trim, dark-haired young lady with the alligator violin case from the start. But there was no time in Frank Wilbur Chace's orchestra class to think of love at first sight.

XIV

Two Years at Boulder

"If he could do it, I can do it," was certainly my aim when I entered the University of Colorado at Boulder. My dad was a self-made man, something I was not allowed to forget. Do not forget, either, that he had been twenty-three when he entered Stanford and I was seventeen when I entered Boulder. Nevertheless, I look back upon having made a good stab at it.

At UC Boulder, where I was a freshman in 1925, I took the English course requirement in composition. I escaped the one called "Dumbbell English" by the students. Nevertheless, *Smart's Handbook* was the text and my papers in composition had the appearance of smallpox most of the first term. George F. Reynolds, my adviser and English Department chairman, believed that I should aim toward journalism, narrowed specifically toward musical criticism, after he discovered my music interests. It seemed logical at the time.

I promptly signed up for Professor Reynold's famous course in the facts and backgrounds of English literature. His text contained a map of London. It was too many years later that my second wife Dorothy and I visited London for it to have been very helpful on that trip. However, I have appreciated his teaching and personality in later years and will always do so. What a man!

George Reynolds was a sophisticated but utterly humane professor who lived and breathed his subject. I made his 8:00 A.M. class on time regularly, sometimes without breakfast, after shoveling snow and stoking furnaces for two or more hours beforehand. Dr. Reynolds's lectures were usually delivered while he sat on the edge of the stage in the Little Theater in Old Main and tied and untied his shoelaces.

My freshman year also included Dr. Reynolds's course in biblical backgrounds, interesting and often spellbinding. I was always wide awake in class, regardless of fatigue from my early morning work. By Christmastime, playing in the theater accentuated my problem.

All of Dr. Reynolds's students adored him, and one of my regrets when we moved to the coast was to be deprived of our association.

•   •   •

Trios were definitely in the picture during my sophomore year at Boulder. A new little theater was built that had a small pit in front of the stage. This small cement hole was just large enough to accommodate an upright piano and two string players, violin and cello. Dr. Reynolds, in charge of the dedication and principal speaker, called me at the Phi Tau house.

"If you would be able to squeeze yourselves into the tiny pit?" he asked, dubious about having any music at all.

"Leave it to me," I told him. I had wanted to do something for my mentor but had thought it might look like apple polishing.

Trios, trios, trios, this was the combination that fit into small places. Gladys, my violinist girlfriend, and I had "squeezed in," as Dr. Reynolds put it, in a number of churches with the organist and for a couple of banquets with Margaret Saunders, conservatory accompanist.

We went to the new little theater to try out the facilities. While doing so we rehearsed. Our difficulty, as I recall, was to find a second number. "Marche Militaire," in the Boston trio book, was a perfect first choice.

I can still hear the somewhat contemptuous tone of Professor Reynolds's voice when he announced the second piece we were to play to the audience. His remark went something like this: "I was fortunate in securing the services of my young friends. They will play two selections, harumph." (Here he adjusted his pince-nez more firmly and the black ribbon over his ear.) "The first will be Schubert's 'Marche Militaire,' and" (with a long-*ai* sound), then harumph again, along with a pause and a slight frown and another harumph—" 'Caressing Butterfly,' by J. S. Zamesnik."

What a grave disappointment I was to my distinguished professor. " 'Caressing Butterfly,' " I can still hear him say it. What was wrong with it? It was a good piece of music, not great, but good. Zamesnik wrote many fine pieces for the theater. In choosing music, I learned from that experience, one should be careful about appropriateness of both the title and the composer. Both should be appropriate for the occasion.

•   •   •

Newcomer, Andrews, and Hall were co-authors of *Twelve Centuries of English Poetry and Prose,* a high school text from which we gained access to British writers. Later, at Stanford, Howard Judson Hall was my adviser, as George F. Reynolds had been at Boulder. Steinbeck's instructor in English, Edythe Merilees, taught a course in writing the short story, which was open to students only after a conference and submission of a sample of their own writing.

Miss Merilees accepted me as a student. I felt very strongly that I wanted the course, but Mr. Hall would not budge in signing me up for the full gamut of English "survey" courses, even though I had read most of the writers in the survey courses at Boulder.

I was thoroughly disappointed in Howard Judson Hall. I took his eight o'clock course in Wordsworth and couldn't decide which was the greater bore, the poet or the professor. But sixty years or so later, one cannot change the face of things. His requirement, that we write out 100 lines of Wordsworth's "Tinturn Abbey" in the final examination, seems ridiculous and not a little bit cruel, even at this distance. One hundred lines, beginning: "When oft in lonely rooms and mid the din of towns and villages..." I crammed, spent a sleepless night, and wrote out the lines the next morning. Above I wrote the only part I recall. I do recall the young man who continued to read the *Dippy* after the sermon began. He was dismissed from class. Perhaps I should have joined him.

XV

Stanford

On a sunny afternoon in the fall of 1929, shortly before the opening of the university, I entered the front hall of 583 Salvatierra to find my mother in an unusually ebullient mood.

"I've just had an applicant for your room," she told me. "I liked him and I believe you will, too."

Dad was a professor at Stanford by this time. The folks did not need to rent out rooms, but it seemed like a good idea with both me and my sister in school. Many years before, while living in the same kind of big house a block closer to the Quad, Mother had resorted to renting out rooms to bolster the exchequer. They had lived on an instructor's salary, not a professor's, then. But back to 1929, when I was expecting to have a roommate in the sleeping-porch room at the head of the stairs.

"Mother is a social butterfly," Jeanne, my sister, was fond of saying. I trusted Mother implicitly about people.

"He'll be back before four this afternoon. He wants to meet you," she went on. The new roommate was decided on, I knew. I also knew that I would be pleased.

"When he saw your cello by the piano and I told him it was yours, he said, 'I'll take the room,' " she added. "He's not a music major, though. Says he likes the finer things of life too well."

I went on upstairs to put away some texts I had bought at the bookstore. I did not see Mother again until later that afternoon. Dan Bryant was at the door. I showed him what was to be our abode, our study room with two desks with gooseneck study lamps on each, straight chairs, armchair, and a closet with steps leading to the huge attic. Another door led to the screened-in sleeping porch with two cots upon which we were to sleep.

Especially I liked the fact that he was a violinist. He was tall, serious, and personable, a Baptist minister's son. As a park ranger, Dan had been guiding tourists through the Oregon caves during the summer. It was easy to visualize him in a ranger's outfit. I liked my new roommate immediately but learned enough about him to impress me in a few weeks, as he was learning about me. He had been concertmaster of the Oregon State Orchestra under Marguerite McManus, a former Auer student in Russia and a student of Caesar Thompson in the States. Dan soon met my friends Elwyn Bugge, tennis and fencing coach (also violinist), and Bourne G. Eaton, physics major (plus oboe, sax, and clarinet) from Greeley and Boulder and former Coloradan close friend.

Dan Bryant had the mission and spirit, probably a gift from his father. He soon discovered Leo Matesky, a Jewish fellow who shortly became his man Friday. Leo sang, tap-danced, and had been in vaudeville for a year between high school and college. An unlikely associate for Dan, one might say, but this relationship lasted for many years after Stanford. In later years both lived in the Los Angeles area, Leo managing a furniture store, Dan becoming a lawyer and later joining the Bekins Van and Storage Company and finally becoming president and general manager. When Leo and his wife divorced, Leo sought out old friend Dan Bryant to represent him.

All of these fellow students at Stanford were frequent visitors to Dan's and my room, the second-floor sleeping-porch room at 583 Salvatierra. Except for Leo, all of us were the founders of the Stanford Symphony Orchestra, which, to the best of my knowledge, has continued to the present. In 1930, the orchestra took shape with Dan Bryant as the conductor, Elwyn Bugge as concertmaster, B. G. Eaton as first oboe and stage director, and yours truly as principal cellist and personnel director, or whatever. The transportation I provided for bass viol players and their instruments should also be mentioned.

Dan was on the Stanford debating team. His father soon moved from Corvallis, Oregon, to Eagle Rock, California, and supplied his son with arguments on a question about "theistic belief." I'm sorry not to be able to state the proposition debated. However, Dan had the "negative" atheistic side in the debate.

XVI
Vocational Choice

Graduating in English from Stanford in 1929, at the beginning of the Great Depression, I was forced to make a decision about my future vocation. It was a poor time to try to launch any career. I had sent for the music school catalogs after graduating from high school and had then rejected the idea of a playing career. A master's degree in English entailed study of another language, preferably German, and Anglo-Saxon. I had found the French requirement for the English degree somewhat distasteful and did not want to spend most of my time with other languages. On the other hand, the English degree opened other options: law, journalism, and education were first choices but required too much time.

At age twenty-one, with the Great Depression already in full swing, I was obliged to make a number of important decisions. At first I had not wanted to teach, but when I discovered that I could qualify for a credential in one year by taking a full program of courses in education, I was willing to settle for a teaching career, despite the idea of spending most of my time grading sophomore themes or making out tests for reading comprehension and grading them. I changed my mind about law and journalism.

I knew that if I taught, secondary school appealed to me most. My practice teaching in Palo Alto High School had been in English, six weeks of *Ivanhoe*, by Sir Walter Scott and six weeks with Mr. Matthews and the high school orchestra. In the latter I learned that (1) conducting a good high school orchestra could be fun; and (2) making music indirectly, by using the baton and my eyes and ears, I had discovered another form of musical art, which was dynamic and highly enjoyable, in addition to my cello playing. While I had not previously aspired to be a conductor, this aspect of instrumental music teaching was attractive.

Literature is wonderful when one is not required to be too analytical. I recalled *Silas Marner* with Lucy McLane in my own high school days. We were required to discuss every chapter in closest detail. Perhaps I was not mature enough to enjoy prying into the motivation of each character in the book, which was obviously my teacher's favorite. Lucy McLane moved from Greeley, Colorado, to retire in Pacific Grove, California, where we encountered each other several times in later years. She did some very good writing herself. In fact, she wrote *A Piny Paradise*, a history of this Methodist-founded community, well researched and well written, containing many early photographs. I was proud of my early teacher and friend when I read her book.

No, what I wanted to teach was instrumental music, a dynamic subject: in it one could easily find more to learn every day of his life. There also would be greater leeway in choice of material to study. Each instrument I would teach was a life work by itself. As Gregor Piatigorsky remarked in his autobiography, *Cellist*, every day when he sat down to practice, he learned something new.

Harold Benjamin, author of *The Saber Tooth Curriculum*, a noted Stanford professor (later to head the Education Department at the University of Maryland, where they named a building after him, bless his memory!), my adviser, had arranged for the six weeks with Mr. Matthews and his Palo Alto High School Orchestra. This practice teaching was an important introduction to my future vocation.

What were my most valuable first experiences in this field? Certainly I cannot forget the ten-minute intermission spent on the Quad near the entrance to Memorial Church, in a joint service with Norval Church, my very first conducting experience, my first time to read a score, my first time to wave a baton, my first time to correct fingerings en masse, to change bowings. All of it was a bit overwhelming—that first time—but I knew I loved it.

· · ·

Teaching a high school band in a California school always involves marching in parades, as I learned when I began teaching. My orchestra teaching colleague at Roosevelt High in Fresno in 1930 was Will Wacaser. He had trained the orchestra there for three years, from the opening of the new school. He shied away from becoming the bandmaster because he lacked any marching experience. As the first bandmaster at Roosevelt, I took over a group of wind and percussion players already trained to play their instruments, a ready-made band.

Wacaser was himself a string-oriented teacher, but his work had made a performing group possible immediately. After teaching them a few marches, I took them out-of-doors to give them fundamental marching training based on my own marching experience in Greeley, in Boulder, and at Stanford. Because they did not have uniforms, the band actually marched very little, but they played in the stands for the Roughriders' football games. I concentrated on performance and soon had a very respectable group.

Friday night football games became a regular part of the routine for the new music man. I was puzzled by some of the unorthodox things that went on in the school. For instance, Vice Principal Lafayette Hyde, responsible for school discipline, put the bad boys to bed in a dark room for punishment. The school principal showed movies during classtime, permitting students to leave their classes, if they possessed the requisite dime, to attend. He apparently had the sanction of the school department to carry on this lucrative program. He had, in fact, in three years built up the student body fund to $27,000, and who do you suppose had the right to spend any of it?

I was not surprised to learn that this illustrious entrepreneur lost his job when he tried to dismiss his bandmaster, Major Dillon, as he had me. His trouble was that he waited until Dillon's second year, when Dillon was up for tenure. With the help of the parents of his band students the major kept his job and the principal lost his. He changed to a smaller town, south of Fresno.

It may sound arrogant, but I have no apologies for my first year of teaching, including my first band, the seven young cellists I started by working on Saturday, whom I turned over to Malcolm Davison, of Fresno. Malcolm was my predecessor as a cellist at Stanford, my successor in Fresno.

Lottie and Leland, Washington, D.C., 1919.

Leland with first cello and Mother's original piano: Greeley, Colorado.

Leland and sister Jeanne on 17 Mile Drive near Carmel, California, 1928.

Exeter High School Band—Mooney's Grove, Tulare County, 1933.

Exeter High School Band, 1935–36—had no uniforms until state law was changed.

The author, 1943.

Peter Borgquist, bassoonist for McClatchy High School, now professor of music at University of Oregon.

Saclti Orchestra, 1947–48, "Centennial Festival Tour."

Part of string section, Sacramento Philharmonic—Gladys is inside first stand violin; Barbara is left rear, playing second violin.

The author as soloist for Sacramento Saturday Club, 1945.

Sacramento trio: author, cello; Gladys Long, violin; Rosalie Brandt, piano.

Arnold Schönberg—at Montecito near Santa Barbara, August 1948.

Dorothy Murch Long

The author, San Miguel Allende, Mexico, sabbatical year, 1966–67.

Barbara Long Bloom and Michael Bloom, Amsterdam, 1970.

Leland and Dorothy, Mexico, 1967.

Lake Atitlah, Guatemala.

Edna and Barbara.

Friend and colleague Norman Lamb, with viola.

Granddaughter Sue Abdi, who writes lyrics for rock music.

Daniel Moreno, great-grandson, a heavy metal drummer.

XVII

A Trio Concert

Playing engagements came thick and fast after the Longs, Gladys and I, now married, arrived in Fresno in the fall of 1930. We played trios for the opening teachers' meeting. Paul Santa Emma, former Sousa band trumpeter and leader of the Fresno Tech Band, was also asked to solo. Mrs. Newt Bramblett, wife of the well known tennis champion and a vocal teacher at Roosevelt High, where I was to be the new bandmaster, accompanied both Mr. Santa Emma and our trio.

Mr. Santa Emma, a handsome Italian wearing a dark suit with a white carnation in his buttonhole, gave a highly emotional dramatic reading of "Traumerei" by Schumann, punctuated by his audible complaints about his lack of breath and his gasps for breath during rests in the music. We played in our best style but could in no way compete with these highfalutin dramatics.

In the next few weeks Warren Alden, Stanford organist, introduced me to Mrs. Harry Coffee, wife of the owner of Fresno's leading men's clothing store. She was president of Fresno's music society and a sister of Louis Newman, a New York rabbi noted for his poetry. Gladys and I played trios with her. We performed the Schubert B-flat trio for the music society without remuneration.

Also, within a month following the opening of school I was busier than I had ever been before in my entire life. At school I was conducting my new band, teaching two sophomore English classes and a vocal class of sixty seventh-graders, as we were also connected to the junior high school. Since that did not seem to be enough for the new teacher being bossed by an egomaniac administrator, I was asked to direct an activity class, a harmonica band.

I am proud to say I survived this planned mayhem for beginning teachers. My escape and relief, oddly enough, were accomplished through taking on more moonlighting work outside of school. I began to teach a private class of cellos. Individual teaching was always fun for me.

Then there was trio and quartet playing. Truman Hutton was the best student violinist at Fresno State College his senior year. His teacher, Samuel Hungerford, was concertmaster of the Fresno Philharmonic. Sam asked Tru to play viola, Gladys to play second violin, and me to play cello. Voilà, the Fresno String Quartet was organized. Hungerford was a remarkable violinist and teacher. When a concert artist came to town and performed his program, Hungerford a week or two later would perform the exact repertoire. He usually made you say, "You know, I think Sam played the concerto [or whatever concert piece] better."

One day Tru called our home. Gladys and I had rented a small house in easy walking distance of the school.

"Lee, would you like to play some trios for the teachers' institute in Tulare County next week?" he asked. Institute time for teachers was the following week. On the day before Thanksgiving, 1930, Tru, Paul Sheldon, the pianist, and I were driving south from Fresno to Visalia, about fifty miles, to play a trio concert of about one half hour in length to close the three-day teachers' institute.

Our rehearsal, the previous afternoon, had necessarily been very brief. Both young men were competent and I felt very comfortable playing with them. Tru had played on boats of the Dollar line. Paul, also a college senior, had performed with orchestra.

We wore tuxedos and heavy overcoats. Still we were

chilled to the bone when we piled out of the car near the Fox Movie Theater in Visalia. We walked down the aisle of a full theater and up the steps to a tiny baby grand, easily a quarter-tone low in pitch. We shed our coats, undressed the fiddle and cello offstage, and stepped out into the spotlight without any opportunity to warm up. It was cold on that stage only briefly. We generated inner warmth quickly, and our music took on appropriate warmth and feeling as we gained confidence in what we were doing.

From "Marche Militaire" and "Moment Musicale" by Schubert, on through our "New Moon Selection" to Zez Confrey's "Dizzy Fingers," our playing seemed to warm up and please the audience. Even Schumann's "Warum," our enigmatic number, seemed to work for us. My young companions in crime gave a fine account of themselves. (Truman and I were on stage later that year with Daniel Popovich and the Fresno Philharmonic. He later became supervisor of instrumental music in Los Angeles secondary schools and was a visiting professor at NYU just one year before I had my sabbatical there. Paul Sheldon's later career was not known to me.)

This inadequately rehearsed trio job, for which we may have received as much as forty dollars each, was important in my being asked to teach in Exeter, the small town ten miles east of Visalia, a place I dearly love, on the way to Sequoia National Park.

XVIII

The Exeter Experiences

How the inhabitants of the small town ten miles to the east of Visalia, Exeter, received the new music teacher and his wife was a total surprise. Exeter was a tiny Shangri-La, a small farming community, in the middle of the vast San Joaquin Valley of Central California. It was the home of the Gill ranch, several fruit-packing facilities, and a number of well-educated farm families who, having moved there in the early twenties, were financially secure and had their families well on the way. Exeter, home of a red grape, the Emperor, also had extensive orange groves. A number of these farmers, especially those with the foresight to raise both oranges and grapes, had become rich.

Many of the prominent families had children in the two elementary schools and the high school. The new young couple, both musicians, ourselves, landed in this Shangri-La of the West purely by chance after our year in Fresno. We rented a small house and went to work to give the children of the community lessons in music and organize a band and orchestra in the school.

There were many surprises. I was to have a community orchestra, with adults and children combined, on Monday nights. A few wind and percussion instruments were still lying around from a previous attempt to have a band. That must have been in the early twenties. Several of the girls who signed up for the high school orchestra played quite well. The concertmaster's violin was a Gofriller. The band, which had to be taught beginning at 7:30 A.M.—a full hour before the regular school began—was likewise blessed,

66

with several well-trained clarinetists. Hugo Phlock, band-leader in the neighboring town of Lindsey, noted for its olives, was responsible.

A further bonanza: $300 in the instrument fund, which I might spend for the Music Department. Nothing more appropriate than a set of tympani would do. Those had their first appearance in the first concert of the community orchestra. This group gave concerts for five seasons. Some excellent players turned out, and we played several standard overtures, with a bit of the *Messiah* at Christmas with that community orchestra. Later high school organizations were able to do their own concertizing and the Tulare–Kings County Symphony soon provided an outlet for the local adult musicians.

Watt Clauson, editor of the *Exeter Sun*, a weekly newspaper, wrote an editorial on the impact of the "music man's" (my) career on the small community. It was a really fine tribute to the eight years my wife and I spent there. I saved some clippings and have a vivid memory of his two outstanding sons, Sam and Jim.

When I visited Exeter for the first time, Walter Smith took me to see three people: school board members Fred Hauenstein and Fauver, both local farmers, and elementary school principal Harold Stadtmiller. Fauver had let me know that I could consider my work a flop unless I had a decent drum major for the band. Sam Clawson, a fine clarinet player—his mother taught beginning piano—became a stunning twirler, practicing with a hoe handle while irrigating, his after-school job. Fred Hauenstein played trombone in the community orchestra we organized. Gladys was the concertmaster.

Walter held a sheaf of my Stanford recommendations in his hand when we visited Stadtmiller. Walt shuffled through them and came up with one, which he read.

"This one says he is hardworking and uses his head," he said.

"Does it say what he uses it for?" Stadtmiller, a jolly fat man, asked innocently.

Staddy, I soon learned, was never uptight, a truly great friend during the Exeter years. He was an artist, a director of operettas that his eighth-grade class gave each spring, and a pianist-composer (church choir accompanist of the Presbyterian choir, which I led on one condition only, that he would accompany). He was studying bookbinding in summer school one year and bound my treasured Alexanian cello method. In cookery Staddy had no local equals, and his faculty bashes, to which Gladys and I were often invited, were out of this world. He did it all on a two-burner gas plate and a tiny portable oven. Staddy, old friend, I will never forget you.

I taught at Staddy's Lincoln Elementary in the afternoons, alternating with the Woodrow Wilson Elementary. In the mornings I was at the high school. For several years of my teaching in Exeter, the band was scheduled at 7:30 A.M., before the regular school classes began. The orchestra was scheduled as a part of the school curriculum, at 11:00 A.M. Both became regularly scheduled classes in the later part of my Exeter experience. I was fortunate in having Walter Smith as the high school principal and to have all four of his children in the instrumental program of his school.

A part of the Exeter experience occurred in 1933 with the birth of a daughter, Barbara. She arrived in the Stanford hospital on January 10, her mother not having too much faith in the local doctors, although Dr. Don Fowler and his wife, Carol, were the closest of friends. In fact, Don was the prebirth physician, and the Exeter hospital, with Dr. Ruben

Hill in charge, was close at hand. Gladys was a determined young woman. Upon occasion I had learned not to oppose her will. Upon this occasion there was no need, since my own dad and mother, the closest relatives I had, were willingly my stand-ins.

Nothing in one's life can match the experience of becoming a parent. With the new arrival came new living requirements, transportation requirements, and financial responsibilities. Mr. Hondius, owner of the Elkhorn Lodge in Estes Park, Colorado, wanted our trio back (Gladys had played there in summer since 1929) and told us to bring the baby along. We called Mary Geerts, our Fresno pianist, and asked her if she would like to spend the summer with us in Estes Park. She agreed and we drove to her address on Roosevelt Avenue in Fresno to pick her up.

One summer at Elkhorn Lodge (1933) was pleasant and uneventful except for the fact that Paggy (after Paganini), our wirehaired terrier, ran away constantly. Once, I took off after him in the direction of Beaver Point. After the three-mile hike, I felt too tired for the return trip, so I rented a saddle horse from a Beaver Point stable and arrived back at the Elkhorn around midnight. I found Paggy the next day, in back of the Lewiston, being led on a cotton string by small children. He had chewed through quarter-inch rope to escape.

During summer vacations, from 1929 until 1937, Gladys played at the Elkhorn Lodge in Estes Park, Colorado.

XIX

How the Exeter Band Got Uniforms

For the first Emperor Grape Festival parade in Exeter in the fall of 1932, the band wore a set of uniforms that were whipped up by the band mothers from purple taffeta. They were capes and caps meant to be only temporary.

The real thing did not come until three years later. To get a tailored set of uniforms required a change in the state school law. Senator Mixter, local druggist, took the bill to Attorney General Earl Warren for approval. Warren added athletic equipment to the list of band supplies, including uniforms, majorette uniforms, and batons, which could be purchased with school tax funds. Then the bill was submitted to the California legislature. Previously only student body funds could be used for these purposes.

Walter Smith, principal of Exeter Union High School, was able to persuade the local Kiwanis Club to lend the $5,000 that the uniforms cost so that the band could have the uniforms immediately, a year or two before the bill was actually passed. I recall his arranging for me to attend a Kiwanis luncheon at the time these arrangements were made. Senator Mixter's grandson was in the band, but I did not meet the senator until years later, when Gladys and I played trios for the Masonic Lodge in Sacramento.

After the uniforms were obtained, the band was invited to lead the Armistice Day parade in Porterville. We carried out this assignment for two years in a row and bought a new instrument each time with the fifty dollars they paid us for this service to their community. The long bus trips I recall vividly, also the fact that I had to play trumpet for the parade one year because I had only four players on that instrument. I was proud that the alignment of the band, in a random photo taken in front of the motion picture theater during one of these Porterville parades, was as perfect as I could wish.

Incidentally, Walter Smith's son, Bob, played clarinet in the band and soloed with the group in an assembly program. Bob, in college at UC Berkeley, won the honor of Most Valuable Band Member. He later taught at Porterville High and became faculty chairman of its teachers' association. In later years, father and son paid us a visit in Sacramento.

Although in Exeter I was indeed a small frog in a small puddle, I had an opportunity to watch the democratic process at work. It was certainly because my band needed uniforms that the state law had been changed. I loved the place and the people and remained to teach there for eight years.

When I agreed to a concert of the beginning band in six weeks, Sherman and Clay of San Francisco agreed to sell us a set of instruments. Two parental meetings with their salesman to demonstrate the instruments and show a Mickey Mouse movie enabled me to acquire forty new instruments for the band.

By teaching night and day and having two or three experienced players lead their sections (some might call this cheating, but I had to make it go), I directed a concert of sorts at the Lincoln Elementary School. The addition of the forty instruments at one fell swoop was a boost that the band needed to become full-fledged.

I spent summers in Pacific Grove teaching in the music school and practicing on the clarinet. During the Public Schools Week in the spring, the band put on a marching demonstration I had prepared, doing pinwheels, reverses, and various maneuvers that were as spectacular as I could make them. We acquired a line of majorettes who could twirl their batons, a banner to be carried in front of the band, and a drum major with the ability to give his commands. I taught the drums a number of cadences and put on a half-hour drill in front of the grandstand. The Exeter High School Band took honors in several parades, topping bands from larger schools, including Kingsberg, which had a summer program assisted by music majors from San Jose State College.

Was I ready for the "big league"? I apparently thought I was, because I resigned and took the family to Sacramento. Walt Clauson, editor of the *Exeter Sun*, gave me kudos in his paper. Sons Sam and Jim had been involved in our music program, as well as daughter Nancy. In 1938, Gladys and I moved to the state capital. But first, some more memories from our Exeter years.

XX

A Summer at Interlochen

After teaching in Exeter, the small town at the base of the Sierras, ten miles east of Visalia, for a third year, I began to feel at home as a music man. Married to Gladys in 1930, with successful bands in both Fresno and Exeter, I knew I enjoyed this type of work. I related well to the younger, elementary school students whom I taught in the Lincoln and Wilson elementary schools. I had a community orchestra of more than forty, which played standard overtures, single carefully chosen symphony movements, and shorter pieces creditably in spring concerts.

Paid on a ten-month basis, nicely supplemented by my Colorado job at the Elkhorn Lodge, I began to feel that the music teaching career was going very well. Gladys and I played trios with three exceptionally talented pianists, Evelyn White, Margaret Saunders, and Mary Geerts, during the first three summers. Marion Hall, who joined us during the fourth and fifth, was a superb young pianist. She had taken second place to Dallies Franz in the national Young Artists piano contest in Chicago in 1932 and was later to teach piano in the prestigious music school at Indiana University at Bloomington.

Both my wife and I had had private lessons on our chosen instruments at various times. We never stopped studying and practicing as much as possible. She had lessons from Mischel Piastro, in San Francisco, during our Fresno year and later with Joseph Borisoff, his half brother, in Los Angeles. I had several lessons from Lester Opp in Greeley, driving down from Estes Park and returning to play that night in the Elkhorn Lodge trio.

Joseph E. Maddy, founder of the National High School Orchestra, had been successful in getting bands and orchestras accredited in the high school at the Superintendents' Convention in Dallas in 1928. Formerly, instrumental music was considered to be an extracurricular activity, not worthy of school credit. This change made the public school music vocational career a possibility very shortly before I began to teach in 1930.

In other words, Maddy's pioneer work had made my choice of career, that of "music man," à la Meredith Wilson's musical, a viable possibility during the Great Depression. Colleges had turned out an overabundance of schoolteachers at the time. The possibility of going to Interlochen, the camp in Michigan Maddy had founded along with T. P. Giddings, Minneapolis supervisor of music, appealed to me greatly. While the depression had been a terrible time to begin my career, a new avenue for making a living had opened up.

However, many of the theater musicians thrown out of work by the advent of the "talking picture," had turned to music teaching in the schools. While I had gained my first foothold in music education with my combination of English and band, I felt woefully inadequate to teach all of the instruments, from beginners to advanced, a definite requirement for the instrumental teacher in every small community.

It was a tough decision to have to make, to be separated from my wife and baby daughter for nearly three months, but we made it. Gladys drove back to Estes Park with Dorothy Murch in her Model A Ford sedan, along with infant Barby, while I took the train for Chicago. Then the old Pierre Marquette Railroad took me to Traverse City, just a few miles from Interlochen and the National Music Camp.

There, under the tutelage of my alter ego, Maddy, and others, I studied cello, conducting, various other instruments and methods of teaching them, plus music librarianship. The last, a four-hour job in the library, was to help defray expenses, but, as it turned out, it also was very educational. I lived at the Boys' Camp (in the same cabin, incidentally, that Frank Miller, Toscanini's first cellist, had stayed in the summer before) and studied cello with Walter Heermann, Cincinnati Symphony cellist and College of Music Orchestra conductor. My principal goal was still becoming as musically competent on my chosen instrument as I could be. My ability to play cello as well as possible, I felt, was the key to the understanding of music and success as a teacher of instrumental music.

I am still a bit awed by the fact that I was able to do as well as I did. Interlochen gave me the chance to assess my abilities against others'. While I lacked the theoretical and piano background of music school music majors, I had studied instruments privately and was on the way to "breakthroughs" in knowing tone production and fingerings of many instruments. At Interlochen, I played first violin and conducted in the conducting class orchestra taught by Ralph Rush. Ralph's career at USC as professor of music is well known. At that time he was at Cleveland Heights High School in Ohio. Several of his students were first chair players in the National High School Orchestra. Their pictures in chamber groups were used in the Silver, Burdette, and Company's *Silver Book*, a popular vocal text in high schools. Several were offered Eastman Conservatory scholarships by Howard Hanson.

I encountered Ralph years later when he was an adjudicator for my groups in the Golden Empire Festival at Sacramento State University. It was also in his class at Interlochen that I became acquainted with Dwight Defty,

Long Beach Junior College cello instructor. Dwight sold his cello text to Fitzsimmons that summer. I bought his cello library on a visit to Southern California many years later.

Another important activity at Interlochen was Burnett Tuthill's chamber music class. A group of about fifteen met each week to read masterworks of chamber music literature. He was a fine clarinetist himself and included the Mozart and Brahms clarinet quintets and the Schubert C Major cello quintet in our study. In this class, competing for the cellist spot in a string quartet to play over NBC in the weekly radio broadcast, I won over Leonard Krupnick, a member of the Chicago Civic Prep Orchestra for the Chicago Symphony and a student of Daniel Saidenberg, principal cellist of the Chicago.

Krupnick was packing to leave when I returned to our living quarters following the audition. "My only reason for coming up here," he told me, "was so I could be heard back home in Chicago." He was obviously upset.

"Forget it," I said. "You're welcome to the quartet."

He had grabbed the first chair in the Alumni Orchestra without audition, so I added, "Let me have first chair in our last concert," (no one in California would be awake at the time of the broadcast from Michigan), "and you're more than welcome to play in the quartet." Actually, I was pleased to make the swap.

Unfortunately for Leonard, the quartet was canceled. I had already performed as principal cellist before the next broadcast. Incidentally, Harriet Payne, the quartet's first violin, was later the principal violist of the Indianapolis orchestra. Quartet member Minnie Knopow married virtuoso cellist Leonard Rose in 1946. Leonard Krupnick became an air force major in World War II and subsequently treasurer of the Los Angeles Musicians Union.

From the summer at Interlochen, I felt I had gained a great deal beyond the special skills I was looking for: a perspective of the music-teaching job and what it entailed. In the following summers at Pacific Grove, I began to appreciate the limitless challenges before me. My eight weeks at Interlochen were highly rewarding.

I returned to Exeter, California, via Estes Park, catching a ride with an Idaho teacher. We stopped over a day or two in Chicago to buy a new set of tires for his Chevrolet and to visit the World's Fair. In Sterling, Illinois, we stayed overnight with Uncle Louis and Aunt Tace, my father's brother and sister-in-law, and their family. Aunt Pauline, my father's sister, came into town to visit. The next night we slept in an Iowa cornfield before driving nonstop to Estes Village and the Elkhorn Lodge.

XXI

Testing My Aptitude

At the National Music Camp I felt that I was in the ideal place to test my aptitude against others'. There, as I mentioned, I took private cello lessons from Walter Heermann of the Cincinnati Symphony, a top ranked cellist himself and conductor of the Cincinnati College of Music Orchestra. He offered me the exceptional opportunity of soloing with the Alumni Orchestra, which presented its concerts on Wednesday evenings. The National High School Orchestra, for which purpose the camp was formed in the first place, was the center of attention always on Sundays. It consisted of approximately two hundred high school musicians from all of the states. The so-called alumni group was comprised mainly of teachers and older students.

Following my performance of Bruch's "Kol Nidre" with the Alumni Orchestra on August 1, 1934, under the baton of Adam Lesinsky, Walter Heermann offered me a cello scholarship at his school for the following year. This I declined because of my school job and family responsibilities. Back home in Exeter, after regrouping, Gladys and I purchased a home.

XXII

Tulare–Kings County Symphony

One Sunday afternoon during May of 1937, our callers in Exeter were Harold and Margaret Bartlett, a music teacher and his wife from the neighboring town of Tulare. Harold was then a recent graduate of San Jose State, had been a leading clarinet player in Frank Mancini's Modesto High School Band, and was teaching in the elementary schools. He was assisting Cyril White, the Tulare High School band and orchestra director. I had heard Harold's excellent drum and bugle corps and had been acquainted with the high quality of his musicianship at the Pacific Grove High School Summer School of Music. The Bartletts' purpose in calling was to enlist our support in the formation of a symphony orchestra drawing its membership from two San Joaquin Valley counties, Tulare and Kings.

Harold was very frank about the situation. What was most lacking was strings, string players with good training and experience. Most of the small valley towns had bands, not orchestras. Street parades on national holidays were their chief concern, plus the ever-present requirement of half time entertainment at football games. He laid his cards on the table.

"We've heard that you have developed quite a number of string players in Exeter," he said. "If you would join us, and would persuade your players to participate, I think we might be able to put together a fairly good symphony orchestra."

As we talked we realized for the first time that though distances were great in that area of California, they were

79

not impossible. It would take less than a half-hour drive to reach Tulare from our small town. Also, this was an excellent opportunity for progress toward one of our goals. Wasn't our purpose in teaching instrumental music, ideally, to help students achieve the abilities necessary to play in symphonic groups? At first I estimated that we had about fifteen string musicians who were capable of playing symphonies. Gladys and I asked for a week to consider the Bartletts' proposal.

Although band seemed to be my main assignment, the orchestra in the high school had become quite proficient. It was Gladys's privately taught students who had made the difference between our small town and the others. In six or seven years she had produced a fine class. In addition, there were several adults from the former community orchestra who would wish to play. Harold wanted me for principal cello and Gladys for concertmaster. As an additional incentive, he asked if I would be assistant conductor. Cyril White, Harold told us, would be satisfied to be assistant concertmaster. A series of four concerts was to be given, and his people in Tulare were organized to handle tickets and other arrangements.

When I phoned to tell Harold that Gladys and I would cooperate, the number of musicians who wanted to play was close to twenty, including two bass players whom I had trained. Gladys and I were both quite proud of our group of strings who, as it turned out, made up the bulk of the string section in the new orchestra. Many of the adults were teachers. The principal French horn player drove from Bakersfield, where he was head of the English Department in the high school. The first trombone was a music teacher from Dinuba, and the first oboe came from Fresno. The Lindsay band director, although a professional clarinetist, played principal viola, on which he was also proficient. His stand partner, incidentally, Arthur Nord, who had arrived from Southern California that very year, was a former movie-studio musician. He had moved to Selma, wishing to retire in that small Danish community. Incidentally, Arthur was the arranger of the film music for *Alexander's Ragtime Band*, with Alice Faye and recorded by Phil Harris's jazz band.

Several of the best young players had spent summers in the concert groups under Mancini at Pacific Grove, where both Harold and I had taught. I recall two of the outstanding Tulare students, Roger Nixon, clarinet, and Charlotte Mitchell, trombone. Roger, later to teach theory at Modesto and San Francisco State, I was to see frequently in Santa Barbara after World War II. (More about Roger in the chapter on Schönberg.) Betty Swanson, my most advanced private cello student at the time, a girl from Visalia, likewise spent summers in Pacific Grove. Betty, after receiving her doctorate at Stanford, taught at the University of Washington and became head of the Music Education Department at the University of Michigan. She headed the Music Department at Cal Poly in San Luis Obispo until recently being named dean of liberal arts.

Little did I realize that the orchestra's first season would be our last in that area. The concerts were well received and the orchestra better than expected. An excellent first oboe coming down from Fresno and a superb first horn from Bakersfield did a great deal to raise the quality of playing to a high level. My wife, Gladys, playing concertmaster, and the Exeter strings brought a solidity to the string sound that was very respectable.

The Tulare–Kings County Orchestra, like most of those in which I was involved in the beginning, is alive and well at this writing and has continued down to the present, I believe. My one conducting stint during the entire season I was involved with it enabled me to include a number featuring the cello and help prepare Betty Swanson to play the cadenza in the Ferde Grofé arrangement of "Malaguena," new at the time. She also performed it in the Pacific Grove Summer School when I directed it there.

XXIII
A Kindred Soul

"Get that little devil out of there," Hugo Phlock, conductor of the Tulare–Kings County Symphony, instructed me. It was not a request; it was an order.

His usually sallow face was a bright pink and his voice hoarse when he spoke. It was easy to see that my German friend was very angry.

I had made a bad mistake. I had placed Elmer Eddy, my feisty little cellist, in the first chair in the county orchestra. Before the rehearsal in the Women's Club in Exeter, Hugo had asked me to take charge of the cellos. I had anticipated a personality clash, but Elmer was a strong player and a natural leader. Still, it hadn't worked.

"Where do you want me to put him?" I asked Hugo.

"I don't care what you do with him," Hugo replied. "Just take him out of there."

I didn't know for sure what Elmer had done. I guessed that, testing the new conductor, he had deliberately led the cello section astray. He was quite adroit at such tricks, though he had never given me that kind of pain. He apparently just did not like Hugo.

"Where shall I put him?" I asked. Putting Elmer Eddy in first chair not only hadn't worked, but he was causing trouble, as usual. The funny thing about it was that he was a tiny runt of a kid and he always was the picture of innocence.

"Just get him out, right away," Hugo growled.

I recalled the day Elmer had shown up with both hands bandaged tightly and a black eye. He sat in the cello section as usual, but minus his instrument.

As I was taking the roll, I said, "Are you okay, Elmer?"

"Mr. Long," he replied, "some bees stung me."

I was certain that a kid like Elmer would not have remained in Hugo's class in Lindsey for long. Over the years, I could count Hugo's "kindred souls" (as I liked to call them) on the fingers of one hand.

• • •

"Get that little devil out of there," Hugo had ordered me. He was not only the oldest and most experienced of us, but we were accustomed to his Germanic ways and took no offense. In fact, because of his private teaching of clarinet on his way through town, commuting from his small farm in Visalia on his way from Lindsey, I felt indebted to him for a fine clarinet section in my band.

George Burris from Visalia, ten miles from Exeter (where we were rehearsing in the Women's Club), Cyril White from Tulare, Jake Weem from Hanford, sixty miles away in Kings County, Hugo, and I took turns conducting our combined groups for the Thanksgiving teachers institute, an orchestra in the fall, a combined band in the spring. A German army bandsman in World War I, Hugo was our most experienced musical director. A master clarinetist, he had played piano with a traveling orchestra, had been forced to study violin for seven years in his youth, and in Lindsey, where he taught, had developed championship bands. Since he commuted through Exeter, he had taught a number of my students privately on his way through town.

Hugo had been in a cavalry band unit in the German army during World War I, with such short bow legs making riding a mule difficult. Because copper was in short supply, he had been given a set of iron cymbals.

XXIV
The Way the Cookie Crumbled

Gladys performed at the Elkhorn Lodge until the summer of 1938, when we rented a home in Pacific Grove. On August 24th, our younger daughter, Elizabeth, was born at the Dormody Hospital, now the Eskaton. Hugh Dormody, one of the two brothers practicing socialized medicine under the auspices of the Pebble Beach Company, delivered her at 3:00 A.M. on the above date. Gladys's pregnancy had been difficult. We did not discover that our conflicting blood types, hers Rh negative, mine A positive, were the cause. Mary Geerts of Fresno, our trio pianist for several programs in Fresno and for a previous summer in Estes at the Elkhorn, came to give us support.

By this time I had nearly completed my third summer teaching at the Pacific Grove High School Summer School of Music. I had applied for a music teaching job, that of traveling teacher, and was to start at Sutter Junior High and adjacent elementary schools in Sacramento. Also, Mother, after six months at the hospital in Saint Helena and previous time in the Lance Hospital in San Francisco, was definitely improving and had gone back to live at 583 Salvatierra on the Stanford University campus.

Gladys and the girls and I made the difficult move to Sacramento, to a rental home on San Carlos, several blocks from my new school. During a difficult first year at Sutter Junior High and adjacent schools, I managed to teach a number of ninth-graders well enough for them to play in the advanced orchestra conducted by George Von Hagel at Sacramento High School. One should bear in mind that

Sacramento High in the early thirties had an enrollment of over 5,000 students. With the help of additional teachers such as myself, Conley Plummer, Leroy Deeg, Margaret Heilbron, Myron Johnson, and an assortment of private studio teachers, the orchestra grew from approximately 80 to 110.

George Von Hagel, the music supervisor, zealously guarded the orchestras at the expense of the band, as any visitor to the schools would have noticed immediately. Tom Wills, band director, had kept his group a top competitor in the California State band contests held at the state fair in Sacramento in late August and early September. Through pressures upon counselors and other methods, the music supervisor was able to encourage the strings, to make the community "string-conscious." Mr. Wills's school band suffered the consequences. At the time I first observed the band situation in the high school, a drum corps of approximately twenty was all that remained. Mr. Wills soon retired and Von Hagel likewise a few years later.

My thesis at Stanford University was written too early to show the complete change, but soon enough to indicate what I consider the deplorable lack of public financial support for the school music program that has occurred. In many schools where the band seems to exist for athletic (football) purposes as opposed to the musical values, disciplinary and study values inherent in the subject appear not to be important in the minds of school administrators.

Certainly in this age of dope smuggling and peddling, the value of music study as one way to keep the young busy and off the streets should be apparent. Rock music is not the type to which I refer, but symphonic, solo, and chamber music, the types of music requiring the most cultural training and inherently belonging in a democratic society.

•   •   •

But to return to my story, at Stanford Junior High School, in the Oak Park District of Sacramento, I first located the kind of job I enjoyed, in a well-organized school, one in which the discipline was handled skillfully by the lady principal, Beth Hughson. My string classes were scheduled at my discretion on a rotating basis, children excused from a different class each succeeding week, and the orchestra met three periods a week, scheduled as a regular elective. My most effective instrumental work, comparable to private studio teaching in results but organized and taught in small classes, occurred here.

A few students whom I had taught previously had graduated from the sixth grade into the junior high school. I was permitted to organize my own class schedule, which gave me an opportunity I had not had previously. By putting the most talented students together, my teaching resulted in quicker advancement of the students and I achieved excellent results. For example, one class of five cellists who were evenly matched with a half-hour lesson per week were able to play most of Dotzauer's second book of etudes in one school term. It was a fine accomplishment. One of the five later graduated from Harvard Medical School and one from Mannes in New York and became an assistant cello teacher to Luigi Silva at Yale. Two others became the mainstays of the cello section in the state college orchestra in Sacramento.

I tell this not to boast, but to indicate that I could do class teaching in the public school equal to private studio teaching if the conditions were similar. Among the rewards of teaching are the occasional successes such as mine at Stanford Junior High.

The December 7, 1941, Japanese attack on Pearl Harbor

changed nearly everything. I was transferred to the C. K. McClatchy High School to take the place of James Hogin, the band and orchestra teacher, who had enlisted in the army. Although I had originally applied for this position, I deeply regretted having to leave my successful string program begun at the junior high school level. At McClatchy I was to have two hours per day of conducting the major organizations, band and orchestra, plus classes in theory, music appreciation, and study hall supervision. This was not all. The band had to be taught to march, play for school assemblies, football games, parades, in wartime bond rallies, rodeos, and parades on holidays or Sundays, all extracurricular requirements for the music man.

My reward was to come later, when former students of mine were in high school and caught up to me as their teacher at the upper secondary level. In fact, two of the cellists at the Stanford school were the leading players of that instrument at the college level when Sacramento State College did not yet have its own campus and the Music Department consisted of two professors, Fred Westphal and Jim Adair. This occurred during my most successful year of teaching.

Many of the string players who were members of my classes, some also studying their choice of string instrument in private studios, entered high school and were able to strengthen George Von Hagel's Sacramento High School Orchestra. He arranged for me to come to the high school once a week to coach a pair of viola students at this time. But a number of my best players were soon playing in his 110 piece high school orchestra. Von Hagel attempted music that was beyond many of his players. He conducted Tchaikovsky's Symphony no. 5. I use the word *attempted* advisedly. There was an undertone of dissonance and lack of clarity that one could not easily overlook.

At the beginning of my third year in the community, I asserted my independence from the Von Hagel regime by accepting Willem Van DenBurg's invitation to join the symphony cello section. He had phoned to offer me the first stand, inside chair, position as Joe Coppin's stand partner. By so doing, I let the music supervisor know that he had no right to try to control my means of making a few extra dollars to support my family. As I expected, at the end of my third year, he threatened to terminate me. He did not want any of the traveling teachers to play with the symphony. I was up for tenure but took the chance that he would reconsider his position.

XXV

Professional Growth

Following a decade of marriage to Gladys and the musical life that it entailed, teaching instrumental music and in my spare time working (practicing cello and playing trios or other jobs that came our way), I felt reasonably successful. I had agreed before our marriage that she should continue with her career, private teaching and playing, and this she did. Teachers of her choice, while we were in Exeter, were Mischel Piastro in San Francisco and Joseph Borisoff in Los Angeles. Her playing of the violin improved with such assignments as Piastro's arrangement of "Chorus of the Dervishes" by Beethoven and Leopold Auer's arrangement of "Flight of the Bumblebee" by Rimsky-Korsakov. Borisoff's method of bow change at the frog helped both of us.

Our concert playing was a natural addendum to our study and teaching, or vice versa. As personal improvement took place, students seemed to learn by osmosis.

Since I was the chief breadwinner of the family, my additional schooling was something Gladys never opposed.

The Colorado job in the summers and a school contract in the winter were assurances of our survival, not to mention the security of teacher tenure in Sacramento.

In retrospect, Gladys and I were luckier than many. I resolved to try always to have more than one string to my bow. I was a jack-of-all-trades kind of musician and music teacher, with a "playing knowledge," eventually, of strings and brass. The gaps in woodwind and percussion were reduced by a year of study on sabbatical in New York in 1951–52. At New York University with Van Bodegraven, exchanging cello for oboe lessons, I learned to make reeds and the fingerings on those difficult solo instruments of the double reed family, without adequate numbers of private teachers. Variety is the spice of life, and I enjoyed what I was doing.

Our two daughters, Barbara and Elizabeth, arriving in 1933 and 1938, allowed me to believe that my musical education and experience should continue on schedule.

XXVI

The Public School Music Game

As with learning to play an instrument, one's conducting improves over the years. I came to Pacific Grove in the mid-thirties to improve my knowledge of conducting and the clarinet. Frank Mancini from Modesto, a former Sousa band clarinetist whose Modesto High School Band placed high in the national band contests, was the director of the summer music school. My three summers under his guidance constituted an apprenticeship of the kind one could not duplicate by going to a music school.

There were weekly concerts throughout each summer. Some of Mancini's students had graduated from college and become music teachers all over Northern California. Many were clarinetists and I was able to exchange cello lessons for clarinet lessons for myself. One of the students with whom I made this exchange was Harold Bartlett.

As an important part of my so-called "apprenticeship" with Mancini, he gave me many opportunities to conduct the orchestra. I coached the cello section each summer, which brought me into contact with many young cellists throughout the state.

One summer Hal Garrot, music critic on the Monterey *Herald*, was on vacation and Mr. Ingham, the school principal, asked me to write the reviews in his place. This I did, often late at night after a good day's work.

I have noticed that many symphonic conductors continue to practice their profession until a ripe old age. Toscanini did so into his nineties, and Monteux in San Francisco was no spring chicken. A conductor of school groups has at least one thing in common with the professional conductor: hours spent each day in calisthenics, which are an integral part of conducting. This arm waving, even an hour or two a day, has had an effect on my own longevity and state of health through many years.

As a high school music teacher and night school orchestra conductor, I probably spent an average of from twelve to twenty hours on the podium per week. That was lots of exercise. My physical activity was not confined to arm waving. I was often setting up music stands to accommodate different groups, passing out music, and doing similar chores that were equivalent to four or five sets of tennis per day, I would judge. Let me say that the daily routine of an instrumental music teacher/moonlighting musician was beneficial, healthwise.

Of course, I did other bad things to counteract the good, such as smoking cigarettes and keeping late hours.

Now, when I play golf on the municipal course in Pacific Grove, I pull my own cart and the cuyu grass on the eighth and the hill on the seventh always give me a twinge of pain to remind me of those teaching days and Georgella, a pretty little girl who played bass viol. She liked to sneak out early.

Let me clarify the situation. The rehearsal room of the Sacramento High auditorium was upstairs at the back. It was semicircular, the floor tiered up on three levels to give woodwinds, brass, and percussion their different levels above the strings.

Five minutes at the end of rehearsal were necessarily allotted to returning the instruments to their cases and placing them in racks in the instrument storage room. There were three possible exits from the room, two main doors leading to front and back stairs and a third through the instrument storage room, also at the top of the stairs.

The girls' rest room was at the first landing, the boys' on the ground floor.

An orchestra, numbering fifty students, with dismissal five minutes before the bell could put away their instruments, use the bathroom facilities, and walk to their next class in the main building just barely in five minutes, the time allotted between bells.

Shortly before the Georgella incident, I had been visited by the administration. Malcolm Murphy, the principal, whose presence I had felt only remotely (band and orchestra students were generally well behaved, as they were interested in their subject, an elective), appeared and chewed me out thoroughly. I had heard that Malcolm had been on a bit of a rampage and had lost his cool with the head custodian. He had just come through a difficult lawsuit and was building a new gym, and most teachers knew that he was getting pressure from Twenty-first and L, the downtown school administration.

"Your people are coming out early," he reproached me. "They were clear out of the building before the bell rang." His tone was recriminatory.

"I know," I said. "We have three exits. I have tried—"

He soon shut me up. I could see that his dander was really up and I figured my best policy was nonresistance. He was a tall man with a volatile temper.

"They need to use the bathroom before their next class," I suggested.

"They should do that between bells," he argued.

I thought of the size of the forty-acre campus but realized there was no way to convince him that I was not at fault.

"What should I do?"

That stopped him briefly. "You must keep them in the room until the bell," he insisted.

"Then two of the exits will have to be sealed or locked somehow. They all unlock from the inside, and the kids can get out at any time."

Why hadn't I asked him what to do in case of fire or other disaster? Often there were fifty or sixty in the room. With one possible exit, he was asking for something any fire chief would prohibit.

Despite the grumbling from students, the locksmith changed the locks. After all, the building was quite fire-proof.

I had worked with Malcolm for a long time, four years at McClatchy before this school. I was sure at this time that the principal was a sick man, as later events soon proved.

XXVII

Extracurricular Activities of a Music Teacher

Although she may have seemed to be an unlikely person to inspire the organization and growth of ASTA (American String Teachers Association) in Northern California, it was Lucie Landen of Menlo Park who stimulated the growth of ASTA throughout the state of California. She was a public school string teacher, spending most of her working hours with young beginners. However, in meetings with the great advanced string teachers of Southern California such as Joachim Chassman, Henry Temianka, and the Schoenbach sisters, it was Lucy who motivated the entire group.

Cleveland-educated and certainly a well-trained and effective string teacher herself, Lucy made all of us in the business realize our kinship, whether we were in the upper echelons with advanced students or giving students in the early stages of playing stringed instruments their first few lessons. It was Lucie who stimulated me to start up the Sacramento branch of ASTA, one of five or six of California's branches of the association. It was also she who at the Los Angeles area meetings passed out assignments that were eagerly accepted by the big-name private studio and concert artist teachers of the Hollywood and L.A. area.

A unique feature of the ASTA organization was the combination of public school and private studio teachers for the first time to work in a common cause, promoting the improvement of quality of their mutual students, instead of working solely for their own autonomy and aggrandizement. An outsider would find it hard to believe that public school and private teachers could stoop to such low throat-cutting tactics as they did in earlier days. The ASTA organization was the first widespread attempt to bring these groups together. The majority of members in Northern California were public school people; in Southern California, if I'm not mistaken, studio teachers prevailed.

To start the ball rolling for an organization in Sacramento, I arranged for a Sunday afternoon meeting at the state college. I made a list of forty people who I knew were either public school or private studio teachers. Only five of those I had sent cards to appeared. Most fortunately, one was Dr. Harvey Reddick of the State College Music Department. A follow-up meeting the next fall brought fifteen, a following meeting more than twenty, the required number to form a new chapter.

Lucie Landen paid her own expenses to come from Menlo Park to a fourth organizational meeting. As California State president of ASTA, she was able to organize the chapter, have me appointed as the first local chapter president, and help us get started. Shortly thereafter she asked me to accept the secretarial job for the California unit of ASTA. After talking it over with my wife to see if she would assist, I accepted.

I had previously had secretary experience for the Sacramento Branch of the California Writers Club, an organization of about forty members. ASTA at this time had over 300 members and, before my tenure of four years, had grown to well over 400. Quarterly mailings of the *Soundpost*, plus time required for meetings and my moonlighting as a professional cellist, were all a labor of love. It took every spare moment out of four weeks of the year. We felt well repaid, however, when it came time to go to the larger state meetings and we could rub shoulders with some of the national officers of the organization and leading string players and teachers of our time.

XXVIII
Moonlighting

Moonlighting as a musician and teaching instrumental music in the Sacramento school system became a way of life for me throughout the 1940s and 1950s. Playing for musical shows in the pit orchestras, in the California State Fair Orchestra just prior to the opening of school, and in the local symphony during the winter season were the means at my disposal for supplementing my income. Often I would return from a hard day at school to find that my services as a cellist were needed.

Alex Brown, Stockton cellist and wife of Horace, a delightful Brit with tremendous vitality and wit, called one day in a shaky voice to tell me she had run into a cow while coming up from Stockton on the back road. She had injured both herself and her cello and wrecked her car. The call came at 4:30 P.M., just as I returned home from work. I played for *South Pacific* that night, filling in for Alex, sight-reading the entire show.

Sight-reading can be precarious. There can be pre-agreed sudden stops in the action (and the music). *Rubato, accelerando, fermata* and *rallentando* are names for a variety of changes in the music that can be accomplished in various ways. Rehearsals take care of the musicians' understanding of what is meant, as the conductor clarifies it. Sight-reading can expose the unrehearsed in embarrassing ways. I was thankful that I had come up through the silent picture era and did not inflict my particular brand of boo-boos, what might be called "cello flubs," upon the theatergoers.

．　　　．　　　．

A new wrinkle in musical entertainment that sprang up in the late forties was the Music Circus, musical shows in a tent. The format was originated by St. John Terrell. While in special services in Manila during World War II, he had devised a scheme for making a theatrical setting in a hurry to entertain U.S. troops. By scooping a circular area in the earth with bulldozers and putting a stage in the center, he had an outdoor theater. The GIs could sit close to the stage on all sides for shows such as Bob Hope's troupe.

After the war, at Lambertville, New Jersey, Terrell, by use of high-tensile-strength steel poles, was able to get the bracing out of the way so spectators could see. In the small pit dug at the side of the stage, eight or nine musicians could play, only the conductor being visible to spectators. At first a combination of strings, percussion, Hammond organ, and piano was used.

In a short time, Lewis and Young, who were producing dinner shows at the old Palace Hotel in San Francisco, brought the Music Circus to town. The first musical contractor for this job was Al Modell, a friend of ours. The eldest of four brothers, all of whom played string bass, he had been the bassist-tuba as well as string bass in the Dick Jurgens Dance Band. With the band for a two-year stand at the Edgewater Beach Hotel in Chicago, he returned home to become a bookkeeper for the Borden's Milk Company in Sacramento. While Jurgens stored his arrangements of the "Chuga-Chuga Rhythm" in his mother's basement and purchased a music store in Colorado Springs, other band members, like Modell, located supplementary occupations.

Stanley Noonan, vocalist and high trumpet with Jurgens, for example (we came to know him through our trio playing with his sister, Dorothy), was on the Godfrey radio

100

show and was held over an extra week when Godfrey took a fancy to his superb singing and Irish charm. At Christmas, prior to his being shipped out for Okinawa (World War II), we spent an unforgettable evening playing and singing together. Stanley was in the Stanford University production of *Peter Grimes* directed by Jan Popper and continued with church jobs and other solo assignments in the San Francisco area for many years.

Dorothy Noonan became piano teacher at the city college, played chamber music, and moonlighted, as we did, by playing the Music Circus. I have often wished that we had tapes of her performances of major trios, such as the Brahms B Major, which we played with her in the Crocker Art Gallery. She was the Music Circus pianist for the three summers and more that I played. My daughter Barbara and Gladys joined the orchestra for one of these.

The Music Circus job overlapped the school year. Thus I found myself playing during the first week of school in the fall. As I had played during the last week of school the spring before, I had not had one night off in the entire time. Today the union would not permit this kind of slave labor. The only thing that made it palatable was the variety in show biz.

•   •   •

The element of uncertainty in show business is part of what makes it so interesting to the participant. I recall Ann Triola in *Annie Get Your Gun* (in the "theater-in-the-round" Music Circus) skipping quickly over to the pit to get her next lines from Jimmie Guthrie. Also, when she was demonstrating her marksmanship, Annie's bird, a stuffed seagull I presume, did not fall to the deck when the mechanism failed. After a moment of silence, she quipped,

"That would have been a good one if I had hit him."

Quite a few such emergencies occur in show biz.

Sacramento was the off-Broadway where first performances of shows just "put together" occurred. One such unforeseen occurrence happened in a show starring Ed Wynne, and the audience was none the wiser. The backstage change of set machinery failed for nearly half an hour. During the time it took to straighten out the difficulty, the great comedian was in front of the curtain, in the spotlight, regaling the crowd with one gag after another. That took not only presence of mind on his part, but guts. Finally the set was ready and Ed Wynne could take his bow and leave. Beforehand no one could have predicted how long he would have to hold forth.

Top Banana with Phil Silvers was booked at the Alhambra Theater during the California State Fair. Apparently, Denny and Watrous of Carmel, the originators of the Bach Festival there, overestimated the drawing power of the fair. The Alhambra, a gigantic movie palace seating close to four or possibly five thousand, was practically empty during those four nights.

But the show must go on. Phil Silvers was as relaxed as members of the orchestra. We were out back, by the water tower, playing work-up ball until a few moments before show time. People in the audience, not more than four hundred scattered about the vast auditorium, were invited to leave their reserved seats and move to the front. Tommy Boyd, I believe, had contracted the show and was playing concertmaster to the nearly empty house. It was rumored that "the girls" had dropped $12,000 on the ill-advised deal.

XXIX
Clowning Around

Playing in a show orchestra has always been fun for me because one can be sure unexpected things will happen. Also, one comes into fairly close contact with celebrities and learns "how the other half lives." Some of my most memorable experiences came while playing in the orchestra for the California State Fair for the shows given in front of the grandstand.

I worked for several musical contractors as the sole cellist on this job over a ten-year period, moonlighting of course from my school job. Tommy Boyd was one. He had directed the Orpheum Theater Orchestra in San Francisco for nine years, was an excellent violinist, and usually played concertmaster on his jobs. His original home was Sacramento, and he had returned to live there.

Tommy directed the Folsom Prison Band and taught at Folsom High School. He and Dave (Curly) Burnam, the Sacramento Junior College orchestra director, were a riot when they got together before jobs to clown around. Facing each other, violins under chins, each would finger the other's fiddle while bowing his own, playing some duo they knew. They always made a "lights out" ending followed by a handshake right in tempo.

This was an act requiring the closest kind of cooperation between matching fiddlers. Everyone was amused by their routines, which were always different. Curly was, of course, almost completely bald, with one of those narrow, elongated craniums that dips a bit in the middle. Tommy, a businessman type, was a sly character who would add an extra hour's pay to our checks by boondoggling an extra fifteen minutes in a 2:00 A.M. rehearsal, all without batting an eyelid.

Some of the afternoon shows were pretty sticky. Abbott and Costello were holding forth one afternoon with a little black boy shading them with a beach umbrella while they were doing their routines. It was so hot that I made my round cake of cello rosin into a square with my fingers. It was like putty. You could have fried an egg on the grandstand without a fire. It was so hot that if you were listening you didn't care if Who was on First or Third. But things cooled off in the evening.

Jose Iturbi flew in late from making the soundtrack for a Tchaikovsky movie in Hollywood. I saw his plane going over to the south of the racetrack bleachers, preparing to land. We were nearly through the first half by the time he arrived. I recall that night especially because that was the night Leo Carillo fell off his palomino in front of the grandstand. He was unhurt. About ten minutes before the conductor, Al Lyons, climbed onto the podium to give the downbeat, Sonny Tufts wandered into the pit looking for someone named Dolores.

"Doesn't anyone here know Dolores?" he kept asking. No one paid any attention to him.

Finally Rosalie Brandt, at the piano, heard him and began to feel out a tune on the ivories.

"Oh. Oh, you mean '*Dolores*.'" She broke off conversation and played a four-bar intro.

Sonny joined her sub rosa or sotto voce—whichever you prefer to call it—for about eight more bars and stumbled up the stairway to go backstage.

"S'nuff," I heard him mutter. "S'besh 'hearshal I ever had."

Not more than twenty minutes later he was onstage,

"wowing the customers," as we liked to say, about twenty thousand packing the grandstand directly across the track from the outdoor stage and pit and another ten thousand in the bleachers farther down. Whether Sonny had been drinking or was just clowning around I was never quite sure.

Iturbi hit an awesome clinker in "Claire de Lune," magnified horrendously by the loudspeakers. It was a pity, because he was playing extremely well in those days. Must have been tired. His sister, Amparo, did a creditable job with the Sacramento Symphony, in which I played during the fall and winter.

There were many onstage mix-ups, don't worry. We did a number from Vincent Youman's *Up in Central Park*—a barbershop quartet singing "The Fireman's Bride." That night we were playing an Oriental overture. The four guys wearing their firemen hats, mistakenly thinking it was their cue, rushed onstage. That took a lot of quick "shuffling of the charts" in the pit. They were permitted to go on, though scheduled three acts later. Show biz is like that.

During the week that Rudy Vallee conducted, "Pony Boy," a fast kind of gallop, was the "play-on" in place of an overture. Used mainly as a racket to get the attention of the noisy crowd, the piece became a rowdy, raucous opener for the entire program. Rudy Vallee threw the orchestra a decided curve to assure this.

" 'Pony Boy' in D-flat!" he would yell. Or B-flat or G-flat—he really didn't care. Down came the baton in circus tempo. What occurred was a hideous racket, exactly what he wanted. Hardly anyone heard the key he named. Playing this piece presto on the cello, often transposing a fourth or fifth without time to figure out which, was an impossibility. I wished for a horn or a bass drum to let them have it.

But Rudy got the effect he wanted. I was glad I had heard his Coast Guard Band show in Sacramento. He had some big-name musicians in that outfit, including DeVito, harpist from the New York Philharmonic, and some great woodwind men. Cesar Romero, Barbara Stanwyck, and other movie celebs fronted the band. I saw Rudy in *How to Succeed in Business without Really Trying* much later in New York. His dry but pixieish type of humor always came through. His "Maine Song" saxophone days are not forgotten.

Accompanying such headliners as Dick Haymes, Frances Langford, the Andrews Sisters, and Burl Ives was a part of our job. Spike Jones and his "musical depreciation" bunch set us to laughing. We played the entire choreography of the June Taylor Dancers and the "play-ons" and "play-offs" for Tommy Dorsey one year and for Jimmy Dorsey later after Tommy's death.

The years went on. Tommy Boyd died. Curly Burnam took his piece as state fair contractor. Curly had a heart attack and died. I had played a fashion show job with the two, Rosalie Brandt at the piano, shortly before all of this happened. Rod McWilliam, whom I knew only slightly, took their place. The setup changed with outdoor theater. I played one season for McWilliam.

Now the band appeared on a new bandstand with outdoor theater seating. The headliners appeared at microphones in front of the band. This was the fatal summer of Glady's leukemia diagnosis. She would have loved to play. McWilliam phoned to find out if violinist daughter, Barbara, was returning for the summer from New York.

"Sorry," I replied. "I think she'll be on tour with the Robert Shaw Chorale."

"Let me know if she changes plans," McWilliam asked.

"Sure," I said, pausing briefly. "You recall, I play cello?"

"That's all taken care of," he replied as he hung up the receiver. He had hired Harvey Reddick, new professor of cello at the college.

I hadn't known about the feud existing between Al Modell and Rod McWilliam. Gladys and I had played the Music Circus for Al. Al had wanted the state fair orchestra contracting job. Rod was a city clerk. Moonlighting with this type of musical contracting was not allowed. Al reported him. In return, Rod reported Al Modell for dumping refuse on city lots he owned from his demolishing jobs, another no-no. I am not sure of the order of these and other events during the feud. I suspected that my being let out may have been one result. While I was disappointed, I realized how fortunate I had been for two decades to have most of the cello work available. I naturally felt loyalty to Modell but could not fault McWilliam.

My moonlighting and retirement from school teaching ended almost simultaneously. I toured the schools from Vallejo up into Mother Lode country with the symphony demonstration group after resigning from the school system. That year I received the highest pay from the symphony in all of the years of moonlighting as an orchestra musician, $6,000 for the entire season. Only because I could memorize easily was this possible, since my eyesight had become a major problem.

•   •   •

One need not live an extremely long life to learn that, like the title of the novel by Archibald Marshall, "the old order changeth." I read it during college days and have not forgotten its message: "The old order changeth, giving place to new."

My playing days were not over, nor my teaching. I played in the Harrah's Club stage band for six months at Tahoe and in the Monterey County Symphony for an entire decade after leaving the teaching profession. I taught the "younger fry" during my last decade of four that I spent as a teacher in the schools, a return to what I believed was my fate, teaching beginners.

XXX
The Difficult Years

In the spring of 1946, having completed nearly four years at the C. K. McClatchy High School, I realized that I was becoming a candidate for a nervous breakdown.

In retrospect, this was due largely to the extra strain of the World War II years. It was also the result of a gradual buildup of school and outside responsibilities and the necessity of continuing with my musical education.

The troubles started during the summer of 1935, with Gladys and Barby away again in Colorado. I enrolled in San Jose State for the short summer term with Adolph Otterstein. Commuting by train, I lived at the family home on the Stanford campus.

My father's tragic illness had begun that spring when Dr. Russell V. Lee, a former roomer at our house, a former boy scout in Dad's troop, and a close friend, made a horrible medical mistake (this is my opinion): a high enema broke through the intestinal wall, causing peritonitis. Dr. Lee took off for Europe, leaving Dr. Blake Wilbur in charge. In the days of penicillin, this would have been a brief illness. Blake Wilbur operated, of course, to no avail. My father spent the months that followed dying a slow and agonizing death, cared for by nurses around-the-clock. He died on a Sunday afternoon in October.

Mother, who had been sedated with morphine during Dad's final days, had a difficult two years before returning to normal. A turning point in her recovery occurred at Saint Helena, where she was under the supervision of Seventh Day Adventist doctors and therapy. Mother lived in relatively good health until 1963. She continued to live in the family home until her death. She passed away from heart failure on September 15, 1963, in the Stanford Hospital.

· · ·

In November of 1946, in the week of Veterans' Day, I realized that I had, for a long time, been called upon excessively by the principal and school department. Every short vacation in three years had been broken into for either a school performance or extracurricular playing. The administrators asked for a nightmare of extra assignments.

Realizing that the war was over, I had completed graduate work toward an administrative credential except for one or two courses and had written my MA thesis, "Attitudes and Interests of Secondary School Students in Instrumental Music." I received my MA degree and attended the ceremony at Stanford. Donald Tressider was president of the university at that time.

· · ·

In 1952, after a sabbatical year in New York, while I was completing work for California administrative and supervision credentials, I was especially indebted to Al Modell for the Music Circus orchestra job, not only for myself, but for Gladys and Barbara. Warren Van Brankhorst, who has since enjoyed a distinguished professorship and violinistic and conducting career at University of the Pacific in Stockton, California, helped fill our string quintet in the pit orchestra for the Music Circus shows by playing concertmaster.

After the first summer with James Guthrie, Kutner, violinist of the Hungarian Quartet, and Jack Cathcard, Judy Garland's brother-in-law and big-band trumpeter, were the conductors whom I recall. Guthrie, a flutist, had attended *Carousel* matinees in New York for nearly a year while courting a member of the cast. While studying with Gabriel Magyar at Colby College in Waterville, Maine, I had renewed my acquaintance with Kutner, now deceased. Jack had conducted for Judy in the Palace Theater in New York.

· · ·

Tragedy struck again on July 4, 1955. Gladys was diagnosed as suffering from leukemia after tests by Dr. Blumenfeld, Glady's pathologist and friend from the Ballroom/Folk Dancing Club we had played for for several years.

Anyone who has gone through a tragic time in the loss of a loved one knows something of my life in the next three months. School began in the middle of September and went on until the Thanksgiving recess. The school break did not mean that teachers were free. Thanksgiving institute was compulsory, comprised of two days of lectures and one for visitations to local businesses. The Sacramento High School Orchestra was scheduled to play for the opening of the teachers' institute.

At this time, with the most crucial of family problems, my school organizations were clearly the best that I had had in my years at Sacramento High School. I felt that I should go through with the program no matter what.

Gladys died in Sutter Hospital on November 8, 1955. Our minister, Wilbur Christians, had come the week before to pray with us. A nephew, Dean Phillips, from Grand Junction, Colorado, was the only relative on her side of the family to come during her illness. A sister, Hetty Birdick, and sister-in-law, Verney Phillips, wife of Gladys' older brother, Harry, arrived in time for the funeral at a local mortuary. My mother, sister Jeanne, her husband, Cub, and their sons, Jackson and Michael, came from Palo Alto to be with me. Close friends helped me with funeral arrangements. I had been suffering from a severe case of bursitis and had had cortisone shots in my left shoulder the preceding week.

Barbara, who was on tour with the Shaw Chorale, playing violin in the accompanying orchestra, flew back to Sacramento for the ceremony. She and Liz were there to give me family support. I am eternally grateful to them and the many friends and school colleagues who attended. Many fellow teachers and administrators were present at the funeral. I couldn't have asked for better support.

Stewart and Mary Tulley were especially helpful, coming to my aid in this difficult time. Stewart was Stanley Noonan's vocal teacher, band and choral director at Sacramento Junior College, and choir leader at the First Baptist Church. Mary Tulley was a school nurse and had a special sisterhood with Gladys in the PEO (a woman's organization).

•   •   •

Shortly after the funeral, my most important school assignment occurred, the orchestra program for the Thanksgiving teachers' institute. It was fortunate for me that, even though my personal life had crumbled in the loss of my wife of twenty-five years, the Sacramento High School Orchestra was the very best in my school music experience.

The musical program included the following: Mozart's "Lucio Scilla Overture," the Haydn trumpet concerto, and the Freedman Second Rhapsody, the last a difficult Romantic composition with showy chromatics in the orchestration. I was indebted to the young people in this orchestra for their truly professional performance.

My sanity was preserved during this difficult period in my life by the constant challenge of my music teaching, moving to a new home on 35th Avenue, and planting a lawn and vegetable garden. My seventeen-year-old daughter, Liz, was at home and finishing her last year of high school. Losing her mother was a terrible blow to her. We both did our best to make this critical adjustment in our lives. I was proud that she kept up her schoolwork and graduated nineteenth in her class of 400 at McClatchy High School.

XXXI
Our Stanley Connection

My interest in writing and photography led me to combine the two in several attempts at photojournalism. I sold several articles to the *Etude Music Magazine,* including pictures with most of them. "Steam, Strings, and the Stanley Twins" was one of several sold to the Monterey *Herald* newspaper and published in their Sunday "Weekend" magazine section on January 15, 1984. It tells of our acquaintance and friendship with the grand old man of Estes Park, Colorado, F. O. Stanley, co-inventor of the Stanley Steamer automobile.

Through her violin teacher, Howard Reynolds, Gladys had received the gift of a violin made by the inventor. She was eighteen at the time, and by coincidence it was shortly before I became a freshman at the University of Colorado.

Mr. Reynolds and F. O. Stanley were not only close friends but had a business relationship that was mutually beneficial: Many violins made by the Stanley twins, but mainly those made by their nephew, Carleton, were purchased by the formers' students. Many of these sales were more of a philanthropy than a business deal. The high-quality instruments made by the Stanleys went for the surprisingly low price of $100 when first put on the market. John Fairfield's book, *American Violin Makers,* attributes more than five hundred to Carleton, plus a large number of violas and several cellos. In his elder years, during winters working in the Newton, Massachusetts shop, F.O. also carved a number of chin rests. F. E. Stanley died in 1919, F.O. in 1940, and Carleton in 1955. Howard Reynolds placed approximately 150 of these instruments with his students, Gladys about 25 with hers. Both Gladys and Barbara played on Stanley violins for many years.

In 1984, Frank J. Normali, owner of the Stanley Hotel in Estes Park, wrote inviting Barbara and me to be guests at his hotel. We accepted and spent a delightful twenty-four hours as guests.

"Our librarian here in Estes Park," he wrote, "forwarded the article on the Stanleys, their cars, and their violins to us—knowing that we are always interested in articles regarding the Stanley brothers."

While we were at the hotel, the owner, Mr. Normali, showed us his Stanley violins and a room filled with Stanley memorabilia. Several personal letters and a doll that F. O. Stanley sent to Barbara are still in our possession, plus the violin that he gave Gladys and a shipping box used to ship the violins. The latter held two instruments and was well made, with a piano hinge for the lid, a brass baggage label holder, a central divider, and a chain to hold the lid. A picture of Barbara with F. O. Stanley and Gladys and one of the shipping boxes accompanied my Monterey *Herald* article.

When in Estes Park, the Stanleys occupied their spacious mansion adjacent to the hotel. We (the Elkhorn Lodge Trio) were invited for lunch many times. Gladys and I took our instruments, and our pianist used the upright in the Stanley home. Evelyn White (later Olmsted), Margaret Saunders, and Marion Hall (later McFadgen) were our accompanists in different summers. Mrs. Stanley and the young ladies visited after we played a few trios. F.O. and I played billiards in the billiard room off of his garage or used a dart bow he had invented to shoot at a target. The mechanism that cocked the bow was his own invention, and a powerful crossbow it was. By this time (1932–33), F.O.

was driving a gasoline-propelled car named for Eddie Rickenbacker, the World War I flyer. I was interested that F.O., in his mideighties, had torn the car down to see in detail how a piston engine worked.

The largest number of cars to be produced by the Stanleys in a single year was 1,500. Production line methods did not appeal to the Stanley brothers. F.O. was invited by Henry Ford to visit Dearborn, Michigan. Afterward he mentioned that Henry Ford had purchased two of his violins for the Ford Museum. In spite of their having been old rivals in the car business, it seemed to me that he was more proud of the violin sale than if he had sold the Model T inventor a pair of Stanley Steamers.

"How many of your violins did you give away?" I asked Mr. Stanley when he and Howard Reynolds visited our trio at the Elkhorn one evening.

After calculating, he replied, "I think there were eleven."

There was another, which I learned about later. Abe Hill, violinist with the University of Nebraska Dance Band, playing in the village at the Black Horse Dance Pavilion, sold me his old German violin, an August Helmer (1858). I traded in a cheap violin on which I had been learning. Abe tried using it in the band, but no one could hear him. Mr. Stanley heard of Abe's predicament. The next week he took one of his own make down to the Black Horse and gave it to him.

It required a strong tone for the one violin to cut through the heavy brass and saxophone sound of the fifteen-piece band. The Boulder Musicians' Union, which had jurisdiction in the park, required a large percentage of the college boys' pay be withheld until the season ended. Then they went back to school with fair-sized checks. Abe needed cash, or I would not have acquired his excellent old German fiddle. It turned out to be an ideal size for Gladys's hand, and she played on it for several years.

During the trio summers at the Elkhorn Lodge I put in five hours of practice on the cello each day. I memorized three major works, concertos by Saint-Saëns, Lalo, and Boellman. Also, by taking private lessons on other instruments from the Nebraska Dance Band members, who were always anxious to make an extra buck or two, I was able to extend my versatility. Gladys was prepared to give me a violin.

XXXII
Schönberg at Montecito

Barbara's first scholarship, to the Music Academy of the West in Santa Barbara, came shortly after she became fifteen years old and included an invitation for the rest of the family to study likewise. Before I am accused of jumping on the bandwagon—being a father who wanted to proselyte regarding his daughter's talent—let me say that I favored giving her a more general education because that is the kind of education I had. Gladys, her mother, had maneuvered the additional opportunity at the audition in San Francisco.

It was not until we arrived in Santa Barbara that we learned that we could occupy the Gould mansion in Montecito with Arnold Schönberg and family or stay in other accommodations, which they would locate for us. We decided that being away from the campus, though it involved commuting by car down the coast highway from Montecito to Carpinteria every day, would be better than being crowded into small accommodations near a great many people. Our only obligation was to play in Dr. Lert's string orchestra several times a week. The Schönbergs would occupy an upstairs room that had apparently been turned into an apartment, complete with kitchenette and bath, which Mrs. Gould had occupied until her death in the spring. Dr. Gould, her late husband, I was told, was a Santa Barbara physician who happened to be a brother of Jay Gould, Morgan's partner in New York.

Due to the fact that the house was immense, having required a staff of seven, five inside with two gardeners outside, during the occupancy of the Goulds, we found the space almost limitless. We used the kitchen, breakfast room, and a small pantry and left the dining room, huge parlor, and other wide expanses, with antique furniture and cabinets full of the spoils of travel, alone or to walk through as one would a museum. The European-built Steinway grand—Paderewski had played on it there at the house, we were told—was in excellent shape, Mrs. Gould having herself been a pianist. We utilized it on a few evenings for piano quintets. The phone pad was a stack of old programs of the Persinger Quartet and a music society concert at the house, and the collection of seventy-eights included such items as Victor Herbert conducting the Victor Concert Orchestra in "Air for the G String" from Bach's *English Suite.*

We attended a number of Arnold Schönberg's lectures, all marvelously illuminating dissections of great works for piano, quartet, or symphony, limited mainly to Schubert and Beethoven. Those were Tuesday and Thursday afternoons. I was studying cello privately with Colin Hampton of the Griller Quartet, playing in Dr. Lert's string orchestra, taking a theory course, and doing as much chamber music with Gladys as we had time for.

Dorothy Noonan, a pianist we had played with a great deal back in Sacramento, was studying with Rosalyn Tureck, Gladys was studying violin with Jack O'Brien, second violin of the Griller, and we were all variously occupied. One day we were playing a fairly obscure trio—later coached by Col Hampton—and Roman Totenberg walked in.

"I heard you outside," he excused himself. "But I had to know what that is you are playing. I know I've heard it."

"It's new to us. It's the Lalo," I replied.

"Oh, yes. I knew it was familiar," and he popped out

again. It was a relief to know that even the violinist of the Alma Trio, which he was at that time, could not always identify items from trio literature. I had thought at first that our playing had made it unrecognizable.

I talked with Mr. Schönberg once in a while, usually when he was climbing the stairs. His emphysema was so bad that he was obliged to rest on each step for several minutes. I did not abuse the privilege but learned several things I might not have known otherwise. He was a cellist and had studied with Mahler, for whom he had the greatest respect. Ill as he was, when the Mahler First Symphony was being performed in the Hollywood Bowl, he and the entire family piled into the old La Salle limousine for the trip to LA.

On nonlecture days, I could be sure the entire Schönberg family were heading for the Santa Barbara tennis courts. One seldom sees such a "tennis-happy" family. I always wondered how on earth the elderly man, with oxygen tanks in his room, could play tennis. I was told that, weak and frail as he was, he *did* play. A vagrant thought that kept recurring when I saw the old jalopy or watched them pile into it was caused by the use of the La Salle limos in gangster movies, inspired by Al Capone I suppose. Schönberg did quite a hatchet job on music himself. I wouldn't kid you, would I?

But it was not true that he lacked respect for classical music. He was a very enthusiastic teacher of classical theory, as his *Harmonliere* proves. In his lectures he lavishly analyzed the Beethoven Diabelli *Variations* and emoted over ninth chords he identified in Schubert. Though I had seen none of the dour Schönberg I had read about in articles, especially in our conversations at the Gould mansion, at the Santa Barbara Women's Club, when the scene was shifted there on an afternoon, I saw the spunk of the little man in defending himself. He wrote a short string quartet movement on one sheet of paper, which could be inverted (the score) and each individual part assigned to its opposite. In other words, the cello part inverted became the first violin, the viola part inverted became the second violin, and so on. He spoke of using *cancrizans* and other fairly obscure harmonic devices to make it work. He had created a fiendishly difficult puzzle for himself, sprinkled with the little mark used by cellists for thumb (Q). Conclusion: Perhaps Schönberg was radical as a composer. As a cellist he was the opposite.

Where was the dour Mr. Schönberg I had read about? Egad! I thought of what I had done. Here was the great Arnold Schönberg having to listen to my cello scratching while working on *Jacob's Ladder.* It had gone on for weeks. To me he was just a kindly cellist trying to give a fellow a hand.

But, Mr. Schönberg, who can make a satisfactory vibrato with the back of his thumb? I keep asking myself.

• • •

I had completed my thesis on music interests twelve years before the summer with the Schönbergs. In it I had reached a conclusion that the higher the IQ, the further from the norms one would be likely to be in music and other interests. The brighter the student, the more individualistic were his choices in many things, music included. It was no earth-shaking discovery, but I had more evidence the more I studied the question. The Schönberg children, especially Ron, at that time twelve years old, and Phil, then seven, gave me an opportunity to make a very unscientific study, by observation only, of the progeny of genius.

I undertook the teaching of both boys the game of checkers. This was partially a ruse to keep the younger from dribbling his glass of sugar and water all over the kitchen. The Schönbergs ate upstairs and prepared their own meals but the boys were drawn to the large kitchen, especially when cookies were being made, or a cake, or something they weren't able to have in their own quarters. But checkers turned out to be somewhat beneath their contempt until I demonstrated how to clear the board before one of them could obtain a king, or if I let them have a few kings and then cleaned them out.

After a session or two, I found out how fiercely competitive they were. They reacted the same way to some puzzles I introduced, one done with toothpicks, sixteen making five squares; move three and make four squares. Another was the star puzzle: A farmer has sixteen trees to plant in five rows with four in each row. Draw a star with a dot at each apex and intersecting line. Or make a circle with a dot in the center without lifting the pencil. I let them ponder each of these quite a while before giving them hints as to answers. I considered their enthusiasm for such problems as quite exceptional, and their problem-solving ability well above normal. As for checkers, I continued to have more challenges than I had the time for throughout their stay.

Late in the summer, Roger Nixon, whom I had known in Exeter days just out of the navy after World War II, and I visited the Schönbergs in LA. They had left unexpectedly early in the last week. We wondered why. Roger had been studying with Schönberg, and seriously intended to compose or teach theory. The Schönbergs left before he had completed three lessons that Roger had paid for. Arnold had had a heart attack, was recovering, but could not see visitors. Ron was preparing for a tennis match, having just won in a junior doubles tournament. As a prize he had received a new tennis racquet, and he and his partner were permitted to play with Jack Kramer and Bobby Riggs as partners in doubles.

Roger took Mrs. Schönberg to the match, and I went on down to see Koodlac, a violin maker, about some cello repairs. Unfortunately, he had a shop full of musicians with whom he wanted to dispense. He had Elman's and Heifetz's instruments in the shop at the same time, and had discovered a minor crack in the upper bout of one of them. He introduced me to Gregory Stone, a Philharmonic musician, who took me to his apartment to see a very fine collection of cello bows. The tennis match was just concluding when I returned with the car to take Roger and Mrs. Schönberg back to her house.

Mr. Schönberg had autographed the picture of the composer taken at the Gould mansion, with the marvelous garden in the background. Mrs. Schönberg had kindly consented to ask him to do that. The original is now in my daughter's scrapbook at her home in Leonia, New Jersey; I have a framed copy that has served to remind me of that special summer over the years.

It was three years later that Schönberg died, in 1951. In the fall of that year my family and I were all in New York. I read some of the spate of reviews, attempts to estimate his importance. No one could seem to put a handle exactly on what his place in music history would be. Was it Stravinsky or Schönberg who had influenced music most? That question may have been answered when, toward the end of his career, Stravinsky adopted the twelve-tone row. Schönberg was certainly one of those who changed music the most in this century.

I have fond memories of being in his home, seeing several busts of him on the mantel. Roger, who incidentally has himself become a composer of note, and I returned to

Santa Barbara after a very full day. I had the feeling that I had been close to greatness, to an ongoing struggle, something of which I could never be envious. I felt I had achieved a better understanding of this Einstein of music.

●　　●　　●

"Toscanini is the most pernicious influence on music in recent years," Colin Hampton said to me that summer of 1948. I could scarcely believe my ears.

Colin was referring to Toscanini's metronomic beat. The NBC conductor did stretch the musical possibilities. He went to extremes in both fast and slow movements: unbelievably slow in some of his largos and incredibly fast in allegros. I had been too naive to question anything the Maestro did in those radio broadcast, orthophonic Victrola days. Not until I mistook the beginning of a Horowitz Tchaikovsky concerto recording for a jazz record did I realize just how metronomic Toscanini could be. Nor, at that time, had I heard some of the horror stories about him, one in particular that I dare not repeat.

Good things always come in a bundle, and our summer of 1948, studying with the Grillers and living with the Schönbergs at Montecito, was easily our most fortunate summer since playing at the Elkhorn in the trio in the thirties. Gladys did have to cook for me and Liz, except for lunch, which we ate at the Academy. We were called on to be hosts for Charles Jones, Milhaud's assistant, and look after the president of the LA Art Commission, narrowly missing having Ethel Barrymore, a friend of his and also a benefactor of the Academy, who was ill. We entertained Roy and Johanna Harris, showing them the view from the roof, and I alone on a Sunday morning rode over to Santa Barbara in his Lincoln Continental on an errand. It was immediately following this ride that my "composition lesson" from Roy Harris took place.

One evening Dr. Lert, the Grillers, the Schönbergs, and most of the staff of the Academy were at the Gould mansion to hear Decca recordings of Schönberg's string quartets. We sat around enraptured by the sounds from the orthophonic Victrola, and it was on this occasion, in one of the most excruciating parts of the quartet with soprano, that I watched several good-sized tears descend from the composer's eyes and glide down his cheeks. It was on this evening that I first learned that Mrs. Schönberg was Rudolph Kolisch's sister.

Shortly thereafter, the episode at one of Schönberg's lectures took place when, after stopping at the car in which Mrs. Schönberg and their sons were stalled at the bottom of the hill, I was declined in my offer to take them to the school in my car. She said that help was on its way. Nevertheless, I insisted that the boys, who had accepted my ride, help me verify that the car of the one supposedly on his way was no longer in its parking place.

Approximately one half hour into the lecture, Madame and her attractive daughter breezed into the room, the elder announcing loudly as she located a place to sit, "Mr. Long left us stranded at the bottom of the hill."

To say that I felt both humiliated and outraged was putting it mildly!

XXXIII

Barbara Long Bloom

It was in the spring of 1948 that Barbara won her first violin scholarship. Parents of young musical prodigies are often accused of proselytizing their offspring. We could not be accused of this by any stretch of the imagination. We did not entertain any illusions about Barbara's talent. She had not studied the Mendelssohn by age six. She was learning the Accolay when she reached ten years of age. On the other hand, her school life was quite normal, without private tutors, etc.

The amount of music in our home was perhaps a bit excessive, but we wanted to provide her with as fine a musical education as we could afford. My own general education and inclinations were quite different from my wife's. Gladys deserves all of the credit for helping Barbara secure her scholarship and for our having the opportunity to attend the Music Academy of the West likewise during the summer of 1948.

Barbara actually earned scholarships to the Santa Barbara academy for four summers, one to Colorado College in Colorado Springs with Louis Persinger, and later a partial scholarship at Juilliard. Fortunately she was able to study with Mr. Persinger privately in New York for what amounted to a fifth year. Later she earned a year with Max Rostal in Cologne, Germany, on a Fulbright. Her tuition for studying with Weinstock and Manhattan School of Music was earned through acting as concertmaster of the orchestra.

In addition to playing as a New York professional in various orchestras, the New York City Opera Orchestra,

Radio City Music Hall, and the "Y" Chamber Orchestra conducted by Gerard Schwarz, she has taught privately and at Hunter College. Orchestral tours included the Gershwin Concert Orchestra, conducted by Loren Maazel, the Shaw Chorale, and more recently the Skitch Henderson Orchestra and Mostly Mozart, both to Japan.

As newlyweds, Barbara and Michael Bloom played concerts in Holland and Germany, remaining in Lucerne, Switzerland, where Michael was violist with the Stadt Orchestra. Michael and Barbara welcomed the arrival of their son David while living in Lucerne. They continued their busy professional life upon returning to New York. Their home is in Leonia, New Jersey.

XXXIV

Dorothy Murch Long

Much of this book has been about my first marriage, to Gladys Eleanor Phillips, mother of our children, Barbara (Mrs. Barbara Long Bloom) and Elizabeth (Mrs. Elizabeth Long Globus), who resides with her husband, Albert Globus, M.D., in Davis, California. Al is a psychiatrist and Liz is a counselor. She played the oboe in her teens and still sings in the Davis Chorale. They have three children each from former marriages: Charles Abdi works in industrial property development in San Diego; Sue Abdi, with her son, Daniel, a drummer, lives in Davis and is on the staff of a dance magazine and composes and writes lyrics for popular music while attending school part-time; Lee Globus, an engineer, and his wife, Helen, a veterinarian, recently married, live in Minneapolis; Albert Globus, Jr., a computer specialist and moonlighting musician, resides with his wife, Bonnie, and children, Hannah Louise and Ryan, in Santa Cruz; Ruth Globus, with her daughter, Julia, lives in San Francisco and is a scientist; and Anna Globus, a dietitian for children's programs, lives in Santa Cruz. Al and Liz have managed to combine their two remarkable families and both commute to offices in Sacramento.

•   •   •

My marriage to Dorothy I. Murch occurred in 1957, two years after Gladys died from leukemia in Sacramento in 1955. Dorothy, a former neighbor, fellow teacher, and family friend from Exeter days, had lost her husband, Earl, in a car accident. Mother, Barbara, and I visited her in Monrovia, where she had a home and avocado orchard. To make a long story short, the visit was extended into a trip to Disneyland and she and I became engaged. We were married later at her sister Frances Randall's home in Citrus Heights, near Sacramento. Dorothy subsequently sold her home and citrus grove in Monrovia and secured a teaching job in the Sacramento schools, giving up the one she had in Monrovia. Most of the move occurred during Christmas vacation.

Until 1965, in our new home in the southern area of Sacramento near the river, Dorothy and I had the benefit of two salaries, plus the fact that my sister, Jeanne, and I shared in receiving the benefit of our mother's estate, comprised of the house on the Stanford campus and stock. For the first time I felt able to afford a European trip. We arranged for a Frames tour to Scotland, taking in the Glyndbourne Festival in Edinburgh. We then picked up a small car at the Simca factory outside Paris and drove it down the Loire River, over to the French Riviera, and thence to Florence, Rome, then Sorrento, back to Venice, then to Switzerland, Austria, and the Netherlands, finally shipping the Simca to San Francisco from Rotterdam. We were able to share a small part of this auto trip with Barbara, who was finishing up her Fulbright violin scholarship study with Max Rostal in Cologne, Germany.

We had left the day after school was out in the spring and arrived back in the fall the day before it began. This was an example of Dorothy's excellent planning.

A summer in Maine via trailer followed this trip. In Skowhegan, Dorothy attended the Cummings Art School and I spent five weeks with the Hungarian Quartet at Colby College in Waterville. Dorothy and I spent ten months in Mexico for my sabbatical after her retirement from teaching.

•　•　•

Through the Davis Travel Agency in Sacramento, Dorothy and I discovered what seemed to us an ideal cruise on a small Norwegian ship, the *Meteor*. The *Meteor* could get in close to several of the Virgin Islands not on the itinerary of the larger vessels. We would sail from San Juan, Puerto Rico, on June 20. Our itinerary included a visit to Caracas, Venezuela, and Curaçao, the Dutch island off its coast.

At the time it seemed an ideal way to celebrate my retirement from my occupation of forty years, teaching instrumental music in California schools. My forced retirement at the age of fifty-nine (in 1969) was due to an eye infection I had contracted during the sabbatical in Mexico. While I taught in the two years following, I was forced to take a health leave on account of my eyes for the third year after our return. This condition curtailed my driving and musical activity almost completely for the next three years.

Visits to ophthalmologists, two in Sacramento and one at the Stanford University clinic, were inconclusive. One symptom, the fluttering of my eyelids, was considered to be psychosomatic. At the time I was half-convinced that the nervous strain of teaching had caught up with me.

"Keep your eye open, Mr. Long," was the request of the Stanford doctor when he had me on his machine.

"I can't," I replied.

After several such attempts, he remarked, "You have only a mild conjunctivitis. There is really nothing I can do to help you."

With this dictum in mind, I went home thoroughly discouraged. I knew there was nothing wrong with my head, but the nervous affliction persisted.

With what happened in the next three years, a trip to Europe and two sea voyages (my own and my wife's prescription), I was practically cured. My feeling is that the salt air had as much to do with the cure as the medicine in the long run. All I know is that following a voyage to the Greek islands in 1971, my eyes ceased to flutter and the infection settled in the lids. There it remains in spite of all the advances in modern medicine, helped but not eliminated.

I was able to play and drive the car again. After these trips, Auggie Heilbron called to ask if I would like to go up to South Lake Tahoe to play for The Carpenters at the Sahara. The six months at Lake Tahoe were a new start for me, but the altitude of 6,499 feet at Tahoe was not good for Dorothy. Her high blood pressure soared in spite of medication. I, also, had become allergic to the late hours. We returned to Sacramento, sold our house, and moved to Mid-Valley.

After living in our trailer for six months we were both quite tired. At the time the place in the Garden Apartments behind the Safeway store in Mid-Valley, in the beautiful Carmel Valley, seemed exactly what we needed. It was an upstairs two bedroom, two bath apartment, with storage room and carport below. Best of all, there was room for my bench and instrument repair shop in a long, narrow room below, meant for a laundry. This was exactly what I needed for my combination photography lab/fiddle repair shop. In about an hour I could convert it from one to the other.

Then Dorothy's health began to deteriorate. Our specialist in Monterey had been on the Stanford University medical faculty. He took X rays and discovered that the carotid artery on the left side was clogged. We then took a short trip to Mendocino County, the Heritage House, a place we had enjoyed before. It was restful and ideal for my wife.

Upon returning to Mid-Valley, Dorothy went to the Peninsula Community Hospital for a test, after which she tried to talk and immediately went into a severe stroke. In the five years that followed, she was alive, but unable to talk and paralyzed completely on her right side.

Only those who have suffered through similar circumstances can know the tragedy I experienced. After trying to take care of her at home for about one year, with nurses taking two shifts and managing one myself, I was obliged to put my beloved wife in a nursing home when I found that my own health was being affected.

When a person is placed on custodial care (complete care), Medicare and insurance companies are quick to cancel out. In Dorothy's case Medicare quit paying any of the bills in two months, adding one month more after I appealed. Colonial Penn resigned immediately thereafter. After carrying medical insurance for several years, the entire amount they paid was less than five thousand dollars. Dorothy's medical and nursing home bills were well over sixty thousand.

Knowing these facts about insurance, a teacher's pension does not stretch far enough. I survived because of the inheritance from my mother, because of my adaptation and willingness to learn another trade, and success in investments. My lifelong habit of cello moonlighting also helped.

Living in the Carmel area was also a boost to my peace of mind. The constant threat of an emergency, medical or financial, is enough to drive someone off the deep end. My daily drive to the Carmel Convalescent Hospital, down and back up beautiful Carmel Valley, was extremely helpful to me. I played in the Monterey County Symphony from 1976 to 1986. Weekly rehearsals, with two rehearsals and three concerts in the sixth week, plus my individual practice, were godsends in keeping me busy.

In mid-career I had lost my first wife, Gladys. We had helped each other to raise two children and had shared a mutual interest, music, in addition to our love for each other. When Dorothy and I were married, our interests changed. We combined travel, photography, and other activities. We spent a year in Mexico and had three and five month sojourns in Europe, plus another five weeks in Mexico. Again I was to lose my wife, this time from the severe stroke she had had in 1974. Five years later, after four spent in a convalescent hospital, she succumbed.

Soon afterward, I rented a house in Pacific Grove and installed my violin repair shop. My apprenticeship with Henry Lanini of San Jose for two summers had prepared me for a trade that I enjoyed. My chief clients were in the Pacific Grove schools and the Abinante Music Store, courtesy of Gene Abinante and that wonderful family.

XXXV
A Very Personal Choice

When a cellist purchases his instrument, often his lifetime companion, he is purchasing the voice that is his trademark from that time forward. I felt that I made such a purchase from Moennig's in Philadelphia in 1965. This was my cello for the next eleven years, an oversized Domenico Busan, built in Venice, Italy (circa 1750), and costing $3,500. Mr. Moennig offered to ship it to anyplace in the country I happened to be.

This deal was not consummated until Dorothy and I had visited with daughter Barbara and her husband, Michael Bloom, in Leonia, New Jersey, and spent a day at the New York World's Fair. We parked the Airstream, which we had towed across the country from California, in a trailer park in North Bergen, New Jersey. Grandson Charles, age five, accompanied us on the entire trip.

Venturing north in New England, we found ourselves in the vicinity of Colby College in Waterville, Maine. We drove to the college immediately when I recalled receiving a brochure about their summer school, which had the Hungarian Quartet in residence. I had played under the baton of Kutner, second violinist, the entire preceding summer in Sacramento's Music Circus. Within minutes of a visit with the Music Department chairman, I was auditioning with cellist Gabriel Magyar of the Hungarian quartet for what turned into a five-week stay at Colby and a place in a quartet coached by that gentleman.

A telephone call to Moennig brought the cello north in

a few days. With little more than week to practice on the Busan, I joined a quartet lacking a cello player, coached by Gabriel Magyar. I worked very hard not only to learn the quartet being studied, the Schubert A Major, but to become accustomed to the oversized cello that I had purchased.

Magyar was quite impressed with the instrument. I know that he later visited Moennig in Philadelphia and traded in his Gabrielli. Whether the instrument I had obtained was in any way responsible for some dissatisfaction with his own I have no way of knowing. I do know that eleven years later cellist Gregorio Follari, associate principal cellist of the New York City Opera Orchestra, accepted it after a brief trial, using it on the job in a performance of the City Opera in Los Angeles.

The Busan was not physically beautiful, nor was the varnish particularly attractive. It had a back made of a single slab of poplar, several knots in the top wood, beechwood bouts, and little noticeable grain in either top, back, or scroll. The neck, obviously newer wood, had a nice grain, making it the showiest part of the instrument. The varnish was an evenly unshaded dark brown.

The maple scroll, which Wurlitzer papers declared not original, was in fact probably original. D'Attili, a noted authority connected with the Wurlitzer firm expressed this opinion after a thorough examination of the instrument. Accessories, rosewood pegs, and tailpiece were attractive and obviously not original.

What made the Busan attractive was its playable qualities, ideal string length in spite of its size, and the unusually beautiful tone quality. Comparing my own tapes with those of other cellos, including my Postiglione, it was an obvious mistake for me to let it go. I was influenced to do so by its unattractive weight and size and by my knowledge of the Lord Aylseford Strad cello owned by Piatigorsky, Starker, and others. I believe that smaller instruments are easier on the player. Follari's early death, at fifty-one, substantiates my belief. I had owned the instrument eleven years when I sold it to him.

Incidentally, Greg Follari was playing the Busan on-stage at Avery Fischer Hall at Lincoln Center. From Sacramento's Crocker Art Museum to New York's Avery Fischer was, after all, an appropriate leap for this wonderful cello. It did not surprise me to learn that several members of the opera orchestra string section, in addition to the concertmaster, play on instruments made by this marvelous Venetian fiddle maker, Domenico Busan.

Choosing an instrument is a very important decision for any musician, and a very personal one. Jesse Levy, an eminent cellist who was studying with Magyar of the Hungarian when I was, said that he had tried more than eighty cellos, from East to West Coast, before locating his. Each string has a quality of sound for which one strives, a maximum and a minimum in volume, a palette of tonal colors that may be achieved. The bow with which he creates his sound is vitally important, and costs for bows now run into the thousands. A lifetime search for a bow is also usual for the string player. Unlike the vocalist, who is born with his equipment, the average string player and the artist make a fetish of their vigil to find the ideal fiddle and bow. Bows that I own include an August Rau, a Vidoudez, two John Bollanders, and a Leon Pique.

I knew that I had a treasure in the Busan. I had at the same time, luckily, a Poistiglione that had been owned and played by several cellists in the San Francisco Symphony. Hugo Friedhofer had inherited it from his father, who had brought it to the States in 1905. He sold it to Otto King, who in turn sold it to Max Reinberg in 1936.

•   •   •

Before I closed my repair shop in Pacific Grove, my new cello took form and was finished in 1981. It had been under construction for some time. The wood was imported from Walthur, in Mittenwald, Germany. I had joined the top before leaving Sacramento with the help of Kai Rasmussen. He was my Danish friend and also manager of the Paradise Symphony in which I played a number of concerts. I had purchased the wood for the back but was not yet confident of my craftsmanship.

Walter Nordstrom of Seaside, who had been a cabinetmaker and had made guitars and several violins, became interested in the project. He secured cello wood and made one cello of his own before starting on mine. As the label that we placed inside the completed instrument indicates, Walter did the carving and I did some of the incidental work. The instrument, after completion, required further graduation. It has turned out to be a fine modern cello. I played the solo cello parts in two different Rossini overtures and Offenbach's "Orpheus and the Underworld" on it with the Defense Language Institute orchestra in Monterey. It is not quite as mellow as the Postiglione, but more powerful. It is easy to play on, has a clear tone, equal on all strings, and I enjoy it very much.

Incidentally, a longtime ambition of mine was realized in the completion of the cello. I did some of the varnishing and carved the ebony nut in exact imitation of the one on the Busan. The scroll, however, was carved by a maker in Mittenwald, Germany, and I purchased it along with other materials. Oh, yes, I drilled the holes and fitted the pegs. They hold well, I am glad to say.

The Nordstrom/Long cello is the result of an experienced craftsman getting together with a noncraftsman (but an experienced cellist) to make an instrument. The result was surprising in the quality of sound for a first attempt of this kind. The model was Stradivarius and is true to his measurements except for a lengthening of the bouts, which in no way hampers the bowing. The wood is excellent, the top even-grained, and the back and sides of first grade maple. Having used the instrument for the past eight years myself, I am proud of the result. My appreciation goes to my good friend, Walter Nordstrom.

XXXVI
Now Is the Hour

Another decade has passed since I moved to the Cypress Square Trailer Court on the first of January 1981. Actually, it is nearly eleven years. One is apt to grind one's wheels following any major move. This I did until I met Edna. That was in 1985, and in 1986 we decided to get married. It is safe to say that neither of us was too happy as a single person.

Edna and I did things as simply as possible. After dinner at the Pine Inn Gazebo in Carmel, we eloped to Castroville, not letting either of our families know until the next day. I would recommend this procedure to anyone who is marrying for a second or third time, as we both were. Our vows to each other were clearly stated and sincere and have been kept to this day. She and I have attained the kind of happiness we both wanted and are now in our seventh year together. Her happiness is my first concern, and she proves every day that she feels the same toward me.

Our wedding trip to the East Coast came much later. We traveled extensively at first, beginning with our wedding trip to New York and Florida. Barbara and her husband, Mike, for a wedding gift drove us to Orlando, Florida, and paid for our hotel while visiting the Disney Epcot Center. Since then, Edna and I have crossed Canada by Via, flown to Switzerland on an extensive two-week trip, including a Rhine voyage, and taken train and motor trips elsewhere in Europe. We have driven to Colorado for a Phillips family reunion and back to California through Flagstaff. We have fairly well conquered the itchy foot syndrome, though other shorter trips may still be in the offing.

Edna was able to sell her family home for a good price just prior to the recent recession. We are comfortably situated in her former home in the mobile home park and have made significant improvements on it. Best of all, it is completely paid for and we have no outstanding debts.

• • •

Edna and I are both exceedingly fond of the McKays, Edna's son's family, including Hal, Esther, Michael, and Eric. Hal is an engineer with the Monterey Fire Department, very athletically inclined, who moonlights in several directions. On days off he may be working on the upkeep of a 65-unit condominium complex, working with a fellow fireman/contractor on construction jobs, or taking care of an apartment complex that they own. His spare time is devoted largely to Little League baseball, in which his two sons have become stars. As grandparents, we, Edna and I, have been regular attendants at local and some out-of-town ball games. The All-Stars, following the regular season, have taken us to Watsonville and San Jose several times.

Esther, mother of the young athletes, is a very attractive and, I might add, a very, very popular teacher of business education at the Monterey Peninsula College. She is an expert with computers and recently received an B.A. degree from Saint Mary's College in Moraga, California. Her attributes are numerous, and the beautiful McKay home, near Skyline in Monterey, is the scene of many large family gatherings.

Esther's mother and father, Primo and Lucita, have another beautiful home, in Seaside. He was a Filipino scout for the U.S. Army at Corregidor during World War II. In addition to an older daughter, Rose, living in San Jose with son, David, their children and grandchildren are all in the Monterey/Seaside area. Linda and Max have three daughters, Elena, Rose Marie, and Anna, and a brother, Franco, his wife, Lena, and son, Ryan, live close by in Marina.

Edna's oldest, Ruby Jean, now lives with husband Ron in Southern Oregon. Grandchildren Mark, Martin, and Michael, Ruby Jean's children by a former marriage, live in the San Jose area. We seldom see them because of travel distance.

My four grandchildren, Barbara's David and Liz's Charles, Susan, and Lee, are also widely separated from us. All appear to be thriving at the moment. Daughter Barbara is on tour with the New York Mostly Mozart Orchestra under the direction of Gerard Schwarz. They are, at this writing, in Japan, having flown there last Tuesday.

At the moment, Edna is baking for a combined birthday party for Eric and David. It is truly wonderful to be even an adopted grandfather of such a large and flourishing family. Many happy returns of the day, Eric and David, and good luck with the cookies and cake, Edna dearest.

Sister Jeanne, from her beautiful retreat, the Sequoias, in Portola Valley, often reminds me of how lucky I am to have Edna. She doesn't know the half of it.